Michael Telschow

TOWNSHIPS
AND THE SPIRIT OF UBUNTU

Photography by Paul Sutton

Published by Clifton Publications, Cape Town

UBUNTU

"Ubuntu" , is a word existing in all black languages of South Africa and there is no synonym for it in western languages. "Ubuntu" expresses an African philosophy of life that one may perhaps describe as brotherliness, solidarity and togetherness. An African Ubuntu philosopher defined it as follows: "I am because we are and we are because I am". The individual is a harmonious part of the society and there he finds his safety, his strength and identity. But the society is nothing without the individual.

In the cities, modern South African society, which is achievement orientated and competitive, has destroyed the traditional African way of life. Traditional African society is based on the idea of the extended family, where everyone, a child, an old man, a sick person, receives his part of the whole. Ubuntu, a way of living together and supporting one another.

Ubuntu often eased or even saved lives during hard times as in slavery or under apartheid.

Even today, Ubuntu is the basis of the society in townships.

You can only see things clearly with your heart,
what is essential is invisible to the eye.
Antoine de Saint-Exupery

Contents

HISTORY 8

RELIGION AND TRADITION 26

LIVING IN THE TOWNSHIPS 10

Preface

This book would like to encourage those who want to visit the Townships of Cape Town and to provide them with helpful tip's and information for their undertaking. Those who have already been to the Townships will find further background information and facts which should whet the appetite for further visits.

Working on this book, I consciously avoided scholarliness and very soon it became clear to me that it was impossible a give a complete survey of the township life. The result is a book, which shows a very subjective picture of some aspects of life in the Townships of Cape Town and their people.

During my research I met many open-minded, warm-hearted men and women and I found some very good friends. Those who visit the townships with an open heart and without prejudice will have similar experiences..

My old friend Mpumi Nqogo gave me lot of support during my project and she opened many doors for me. The book would not have been possible without her.

M Telschow
Author

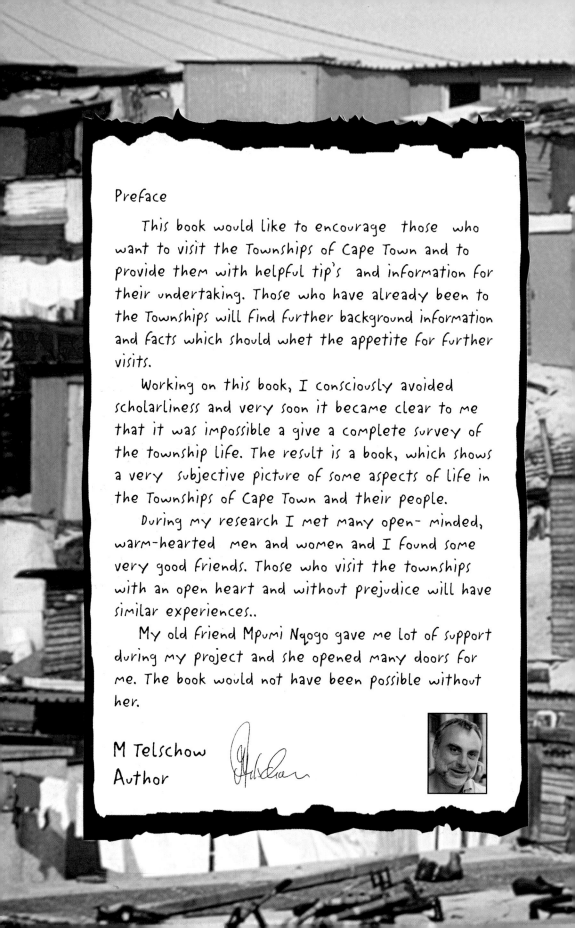

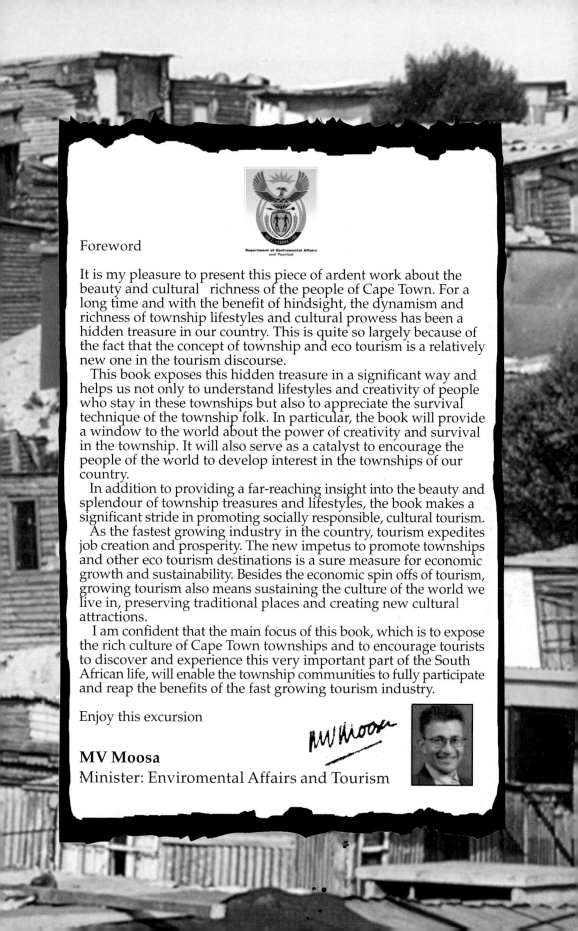

Foreword

It is my pleasure to present this piece of ardent work about the beauty and cultural richness of the people of Cape Town. For a long time and with the benefit of hindsight, the dynamism and richness of township lifestyles and cultural prowess has been a hidden treasure in our country. This is quite so largely because of the fact that the concept of township and eco tourism is a relatively new one in the tourism discourse.

This book exposes this hidden treasure in a significant way and helps us not only to understand lifestyles and creativity of people who stay in these townships but also to appreciate the survival technique of the township folk. In particular, the book will provide a window to the world about the power of creativity and survival in the township. It will also serve as a catalyst to encourage the people of the world to develop interest in the townships of our country.

In addition to providing a far-reaching insight into the beauty and splendour of township treasures and lifestyles, the book makes a significant stride in promoting socially responsible, cultural tourism.

As the fastest growing industry in the country, tourism expedites job creation and prosperity. The new impetus to promote townships and other eco tourism destinations is a sure measure for economic growth and sustainability. Besides the economic spin offs of tourism, growing tourism also means sustaining the culture of the world we live in, preserving traditional places and creating new cultural attractions.

I am confident that the main focus of this book, which is to expose the rich culture of Cape Town townships and to encourage tourists to discover and experience this very important part of the South African life, will enable the township communities to fully participate and reap the benefits of the fast growing tourism industry.

Enjoy this excursion

MV Moosa
Minister: Enviromental Affairs and Tourism

"MOTHO KE MOTHO KA BATHO BABANG"
"A human being is a human being because of other
human beings" - Jeremy Cronin

You can understand the present only if you know the past. A person who makes the effort to look into the history of the townships will understand much more when visiting these places and will see things in a different light.

The history of the townships goes back to 1927 when the oldest township of Cape Town, Langa, was set up in April of that year. Khayelitsha, one of the most recent ones, was started in 1983. The history of the origins and development of the townships is very closely connected to apartheid, indeed, they are a direct result of apartheid.

Apartheid is the one Afrikaans word which is known to the whole world and it has gained an evil reputation. According to the United Nations General Plenary Assembly this term denotes a crime. The history of apartheid is centuries old. Only in 1923 was it written into law with the Native Urban Areas Act. This law divided urban land into residential areas for Blacks and residential areas for others.

Acquisition of land for residence by Black people was allowed only in the territories assigned to them - the townships. In preparing this law, a commission had formulated the principle that Blacks should be permitted into the city areas (regarded as a creation of the white man) for one reason, to satisfy the needs of the white man. In 1948 Apartheid was made state policy. The underlying motive was the total segregation of the races. In 1950 the Population Registration Act was passed and this stipulated the registration of the various populations (Population Registration Act). People were subdivided into white, coloured and black. In 1949 marriages between Whites and peoples of other race were forbidden and, in 1950, extra-marital sexual intercourse between them was forbidden too.

After segregation was carried out in private lives, in 1950 there followed enforcement in the living areas, based on the Group Areas Act, in which specific zones were made available to specific races for living and business purposes. "Illegal" black settlements, which had developed during the last decades and were often situated near white living areas, were cleared rigorously, often in the face of strong resistance. In the townships around Cape Town, thousands of identical houses were built by the government. The people whose illegal houses were destroyed by bulldozers were brought to these areas.

Apartheid also attempted to enforce segregation in the field of work. A white employee was not allowed to have a black supervisor, so career chances for Blacks were restricted.

In economics, the main task of apartheid was to procure sufficient cheap labour. For this purpose, the system of the migrant workers was expanded and the labour market was subject to

The townships became a centre of opposition against government. In 1985 the suburb of Athlone became a synonym for resistance to apartheid. A situation similar to civil war resulted. Police fired indiscriminately and with live ammunition at stone-throwing pupils and young people. The police action named "Trojan Horse" became famous. Policemen hid behind cases on a truck, as it drove into a demonstration. Once inside the centre of the demonstrating crowd, the police threw the cases away and shot at the fleeing masses. With the abolition of apartheid and the restricting laws, the rural exodus continued to increase as the migrant workers got their families to live with them in the Townships.

During the last few years there have been enormous efforts made to eliminate the aftermath of apartheid. But steps were also taken to document the life in the townships during that time and to make this information open to the public. In the former Municipal Hall of the hostel village Lwandle, the Community Labour Museum was established, sensitively portraying its history.

The employees of the museum are very involved, and after the guided tour through the exhibition they love to invite the visitors for a little stroll to see the village. In the tourist information centre Sivuyele in Guguletu, one can learn about the history of this township with the help of informative picture boards. And in Langa the former Pass Issuing Office which was destroyed by the angry population after apartheid is now reconstructed as a museum.
(pictured above)

control by government. The Blacks were split up into two categories:

1) migrant workers who were only allowed to stay temporarily in Cape Town, without their family and only as long as they could prove they had a job. Special hostels were built for them where the workers had to live under degrading conditions.

2) people who got the right to settle permanently in the townships with their families. They qualified for this privilege because they were either born in Cape Town or they had been living here for a long time. They and their families were allowed to stay in a terrace house, erected for them by the government. In 1952 a law was issued dictating that every black person had to have a pass. He had to carry it with him all the time and produce it at any time he was asked to. This pass noted the reservation where the pass holder came from and also the place where he was working at the time. If a black person was caught without a pass, he went straight to prison. But every year more and more people from the rural areas got caught up in the maelstrom of big city life. In spite of the pass control becoming sharper and sharper, more and more Blacks streamed into Cape Town. The rural exodus came to a crisis point where the authorities were no longer able to contain it. In 1982 the minister in charge estimated that 42% of the blacks in Cape Town were living there without a permit. These "illegals" had to look for their own accommodation in the townships and they had to build their own houses. These poor shacks were called "illegal houses". The apartheid authorities had to tolerate this development, because they lost the control of the situation. The townships were hopelessly overcrowded and there were still more and more people arriving. As a result of this, social problems increased and discontent grew steadily.

Migrant Labour Museum
Vulndela Str. Lwandle 7143
Tel: + 27 021 8456117
E-mail:bmgijima@hotmail.com
www.museum.org.za/Lwandle
Opening Hours: Mon - Fri 9.30 - 16.00

Museum Langa
Washington Rd./Lerotholi

Historic Exhibition
Tourist Information Sivuyele
Guguletu

Living in the Townships

*It is not black or white; it is always shades of grey.
And more important, all the grey is moving in a
progressive pattern back to the Originator.*
Marlo Morgan

SQUATTER CAMPS

Driving through a township in Cape Town for the first time, you will be surprised by the variety of architecture and living styles. From the N2 highway one gets the impression that these are densely populated areas that consist only of tightly packed and miserable huts (the "informal houses" or "shacks") with extremely poor living conditions. However, one can distinguish four kinds of residential quarters which differ significantly from one another in their living quality. In the much older townships like Langa and Guguletu, there are five types of architecture.

Shacks, as far as the eye can see. Squatter camps are shabby huts, illegally erected on government land, illegally occupied by the landless and homeless people arriving in Cape Town. These informal settlements have a long history and are a major problem for the municipal administration of Cape Town. It is estimated that there are up to one million people living in the squatter camps and more people pour in every day. New shacks are shooting up like mushrooms.

In the demonstration on the 1st of May 2002, the main demand of the farm workers of the winelands in the Western Cape was for a minimum wage of 50 Rand per day or a weekly wage of 100 Rand. In most cases they receive only 20 Rand or less and that is only a half-hour's drive away from Cape Town. In areas far from big cities the payment is even worse. It is understandable that an average wage of 40 to 60 Rand per day for a casual worker in Cape Town must be heaven on earth to people from rural areas. Every day, up to ten overcrowded buses arrive. They come from the former "homelands" of Transkei and Ciskei, bringing people who are looking for a

break in the big city. However people stream into the squatter camps of Cape Town not only from the Eastern Cape, but from many other countries of Africa. South Africa with its strong economy, its industry and the developed tourism trade seems to promise a brighter future than they would have had in their former homes. The problems caused by this development have to be solved at grass roots level but this needs time and money. With the limited funds available to the city council, it is difficult to improve the situation of the people in the squatter camps, but even so there are gradual changes and improvements being made.

At the beginning of 2002 a foul smelling channel separated the Joe Slovo Squatter Camp from the township of Langa. There was no drinking water and no sewerage system for the squatters who had to "borrow" their water from the Langa residents. To reach their homes, the people of

Above: *Every morning Fayo opens his shop*

Below: *New water taps in the Joe Slovo Squatter camp are a big improvement to the quality of life*

Previous page: *The Joe Slovo Squatter Camp in Langa with the new road*

the squatter camp had to jump from one stone to the next through the open sewage channel.

Municipal administration has now connected the squatter camp to the canalisation system and in place of the channel, there is a much improved clean dirt road.

Numerous drinking water supply points and concrete water basins are available and small grey public lavatory houses have been erected. This is a great improvement for the residents. The new street is full of life and an infrastructure is beginning to develop on its own, as in the older parts of the townships.

The first greengrocer sits at the side of the street, a shebeen (bar) has opened, a small "supermarket" offers a limited assortment and a dealer in electrical appliances spreads out his small stock on a board. The first residents are beginning to grow vegetables in the few square metres which are available in front of their shacks. If you look closely at the architecture of

the squatter camps, it turns out to be very varied and colourful.

The design and structure of each of the shack buildings is determined by the financial situation of the owner, which building materials were available, and for how long the people have been living here. Those that have lived in the squatter camps for any considerable period of time tend to have added, piece by piece, to their shacks. Sometimes these renovations even result in a second level..

Fayo Nyathela, who came to this place four years ago with his wife, started with a small shack. He now has one of the most beautiful two-storey houses in the squatter camp. Every morning he still opens the shed where he used to sell cigarettes in former times, though he hasn't had money for new stock for a long time. Now he has started a small workshop on the roof, the new second floor, where he builds furniture for the neighbors out of old wood.

Above: *Fayo's wife in the kitchen*

Top: *Fayo Nyathela has one of the most beautiful double story shacks in Langa*

Above: *Fayo Nyathela*

∿∿ Semi-detached houses

Terraced houses are found in the older Townships of Langa and Guguletu. From the historical point of view, they are the starting point of the townships in Cape Town. They were built from the 1920's to the 1940's. In accordance with a law issued in 1923, black people were driven out of the illegal settlements and brought to the terraced-house settlements, which were specially constructed for them by the government, and the townships of today were born. Although living conditions for these people improved, they now had to pay rent to the government and this was difficult for many of them. Also, their social structures had been destroyed and had to be developed again.

After the abolition of apartheid, the government made these terraced houses over to the tenants who are now the owners of the houses and responsible for maintenance. However, people are still living under very crowded conditions, and often a family of five to eight people occupies twenty to thirty sqm.

Above: *Inside the Fezile house*
Main pic: *Bunga Street in Langa with typical semi-detached houses of the 1930's*
Left: *The front yard of a semi-detached house in Jabavi Street, Langa*
Below: *Patrick Fezile and his family*

Patrick Fezile and his family are living in a terraced house which has two rooms, a small front garden and a back yard with a toilet. He was born in Langa in 1958 and has been living in this house since 1981. He is the proud owner and has enough time for the garden, as he has been unemployed since 1998. From time to time he manages to find a casual job. Previously, he worked for more than ten years for a company which manufactured screws and bolts. The company had to reduce output by 50% because of a lack of orders. Since then the small salary of his wife is all their family has to live on. She works for a company producing shopping bags.

⌁ Hostels

After the Second World War, an industrial revolution started in South Africa. The developing mining industry and industries subsidiary to it were booming. In Cape Town small and medium-sized businesses experienced a rapid revival. The demand for cheap labour was growing apace and could hardly be satisfied. The answer seemed to lie in the homelands of Transkei and Ciskei, with its masses of people, cheap and willing to work. Since only young men were needed, the system of migrant workers was developed, i.e., men only were allowed to stay in the townships near the cities, without their families and only as long as they had a job. Special quarters were built for them, hostels in which they had to live under inhuman conditions. Ten to twelve men were put into rooms of less than 30 sqm and the sanitary installations were inadequate. Under these living conditions, alcohol and crime were inevitable and frequent. When apartheid and its laws were abolished, the former migrant workers fetched their relatives from the homelands and brought them to the townships. Whole families are now living here huddled in one room. The parents sleep in the bed and the children on the floor, so the children can only go to sleep when the parents are in the bed, whatever time that may be.

Above: *Old hostels on Rhodes Rd in Langa*

Top: *A typical bedroom inside an "old" hostel apartment*

Middle: *Children represent the only wealth*

Left: *The main activities take place inbetween the blocks*

The housing authorities have modernized the old, neglected hostels in Langa and transformed them, with the help of money from the German government amongst others, into colourful "blocks of apartments". An apartment consists of 4 small rooms and a toilet, with water and a place for cooking in the corridor.

These buildings are, on the whole, cleaner and better maintained than the older hostel buildings.

We visited the brothers Sivujele and Luyanda who are renting a room in a modernized hostel for 150 Rand per month. They both work at a carton factory in Epping which is close to the hostels and they are glad that they have found such a good place to live for such a reasonable price. Three years ago they arrived from Umtata in the Eastern Cape. The small farm of their parents did not yield enough to feed the whole family, so they came to the large city in order to try their luck at finding a job. There are other young single people in their immediate neighbourhood and in the opposite block are mainly families. They help one another and their sense of community is alive. This is Ubuntu personified.

Above: *The brothers Sivujele and Luyanda*
Left: *A bedroom in the modernised hostel*
Below left: *A man gets a shave from his son*
Below : *The cooking and cleaning area*
Left page: *The staircase to a renovated hostel*

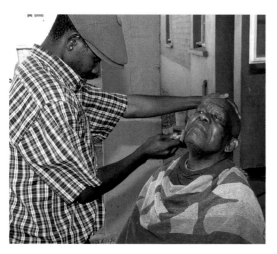

∿∿ Low cost housing

In 1994 the ANC under Nelson Mandela took over the government of South Africa, and he promised to ease the great housing shortage by building one million low cost houses. In his departing speech from the South African parliament in 1999, he reported that 700,000 houses had been built, so the target was not completely reached. As part of this programme, the Housing Department of Cape Town built approximately 4000 low cost houses in the townships from 1995 to 2001. The programme is to continue, and further phases will be implemented in the future. The houses are quite small and vary in size from 27 to 30 sqm.

Anyone who is put on a waiting list and does not earn more than R3000 monthly is entitled to a house. Depending on his income, the applicant has to contribute up to R20300 to the building costs. The remainder will be covered by the government.

The Bock family is lucky. They are the proud owners of a house. Because Mr. Bock is unemployed, they have to pay only R7000 in monthly installments of R150. Two years ago they moved with their three children from a shack into this house. This was a great improvement, for now they have got a small kitchenette, their own toilet and a shower.

Mr. Bock sometimes works on a building site as a casual worker. On one occasion there was some building material left, so that with the help of some friends he was able to add two tiny rooms to his house. "There could be some playgrounds for the children to play on", says Clara Bock, but she is happy to live here and have a secure roof over her head. Two schools have already been built in the area and a third is under construction.

Main Pic: *The community of Nooiensfontein at the intersection of the M12 and the N7*
Right: *The Bock family. The bottom picture shows a ceramic prayer book*

⌇⌇⌇ Township-Villas

In the townships a middle class is slowly developing. They can afford to rent neat cottages or to build their own houses to high standards. In these village areas of the townships in Cape Town, office workers, self-employed people, doctors and businessmen live. Most of them would be able to settle in another region of the city, but they prefer to remain in their accustomed residential areas because Ubuntu is present here. They are often very engaged in their communities and a strong sense of pride can be felt when looking at their homes. Mpumi is an example of this, she keeps her house in neat order as one can clearly see when looking at her kitchen and living room. She lives with her two daughters and one grand daughter in Langa in a neat cottage. She works in the municipal administration and plays a strong and sometimes leading role in projects mainly helping children and women.

Above: *Mpumi Nqogo and her grand daughter displaying her house in Mama Rd, Langa*

Left: *Vokwana Rd in Langa*

Main pic: *The beautiful "Villa" of a middle income Langa resident in Jungle Walk, Langa*

Religion and Tradition

There is only one God in the world. He gave to every nation its own way and manner of honouring him.
Johanna Wagner

ᵥᵥᵥ Religion

South Africa is one of the most heterogeneous countries in the world. Throughout its history, people from diverse parts of the world and with very different religious backgrounds have come to live at the southern tip of Africa - white settlers from Europe, Indian contract workers, black tribes from other parts of the continent. There is a wide range of different religions and beliefs amongst the people of South Africa. Christians form the great majority, followed by Hindus and Muslims with 1,4% each, and Jews with 0.2%. 11.7% of South Africans indicate that they are not religious. There are no separate statistics for the population of the Townships, but one can assume that the percentage of Christians among them is higher than in the whole population. Other religions are also found in the Townships as the mosques attest.

Main pic: *Church constructed from old shipping containers in Khayelitsha*
Top: *Roman Catholic Church in Khayelitsha*
Above: *Mosque in Khayelitsha*
Left: *Methodist Church in Guguletu*

Visiting a divine service

The Christian churches have their services on Sunday morning. Guests are usually welcome, but nevertheless, one should inform the church member in charge. If you plan to take photos, permission is necessary. Visiting a service is always worthwhile since the ritual and the atmosphere are unique to each place of worship. We went to the Baptist church in Langa. Rev. Michael Dwaha is pleased to welcome every visitor, although he cannot complain about lacking members with a congregation of about 500. They are mainly young people and 200 of them are very active. The minister is particularly proud of his youth choir which in 2002 was invited by the English partner- congregation to the UK . During the two- week trip they gave successful concerts at many churches. With the aid of their partner-congregation "Hope Now Ministries", a new and beautiful church was built in Langa and opened in August 2001. The old church building had become too small for the rapidly increasing parish. It is now rented out for events and in this way, it helps to improve the meagre budget.

The church runs two projects, which "show God in action" as Rev. Michael Dwaha puts it. In the first project, a warm meal is prepared three times a week for 700 needy people in their own soup kitchen. In the second one, women of Langa can participate in a sewing course at sewing machines, also donated by the UK congregation. 7.5% of the Sunday collection flows into these projects.

The well-attended service begins with music and the singing of the congregation. Then the pastor says the words of the communion service. The sermon is full of emotion and gestures, frequently interrupted by songs performed by the choir and a small band. Full of enthusiasm, the congregation joins in their songs and moves and dances in the rhythm of thegospel music.

The big, powerful, dancing choir finally includes everyone present, and it is a glorious celebration, a tremendous experience. After the sermon Nona is allowed on the podium, because she was sick for a long time and her mother came from Gauteng to look after her. Today they pray specially for her and thank God for her recovery.

Main pic: *The hymn is projected against the wall for congregation to sing along*

Top right: *The choir of the church*

Bottom right: *Baptist Church, Langa*

Baptist Church
Reverend Michael Douglas
PO Box 61
Washington Rd / Sandile Street
Langa 7455
Tel: +27(0)21 6942177
Service: Sunday: 9.30-13.30

Ancestors and Community

The ancestors play an important part in the spiritual and cultural life of nations and tribes, not only in South Africa but in the whole of Africa. The ancestors are the upholders and retainers of the tradition, the spiritual roots of a nation, and they are the intermediaries between our world and the world of the Gods and spirits. People with requests and problems do not immediately turn to the chief but report the request to the ancestors as mediator. They ask, for instance, if their planned activities are good or feasible. They want to know if what they are intending to do is in accordance with their own culture and tradition, and whether the forefathers would have acted in the same way. Denying or ignoring the ancestors in order to live a modern life, to avoid being called "old-fashioned", means to deny and thus lose the cultural roots of their nation, of the tribe. Often such people feel uneasy, fall ill, as if punished by the ancestors.

Johanna Wagner, a European physician, who studied the secrets of the traditional African healer in West Africa, writes about this phenomenon in her book. She helped many Africans who lived in

made for the ancestors by brewing umgqombothi, and by slaughtering animals. The meat is prepared at open fire- places, because the ancestors eat the smoke. Not only do the people turn to the ancestors, but the ancestors also contact the people in night and day dreams, in which they give messages and advice. These ancestors are a part of life itself, and they give support and safety to the community because they are the roots. In 1999, the Sahazu Communication (Pty) Ltd. Conducted research into the development of Khayelitsha and found out that 86% of all inhabitants of this township were born in the Eastern Province. In Site C of Khayelitsha, more than 50% of the people come from the area around Lady Frere and in Site B more than 50% from Cala. This shows that people with the same roots, the same customs and rites, go out of their way to live together, even away from home.

Main pic: *Group of traditional healers from Langa*
Below: *Njanda N Mhlekude, chairperson of Sakhisizwe Cultural Women of Langa*

modern cities and thought that their traditions were obsolete. She *treate*d these problems and diseases by re-awakening the patients to the old traditional African ways, and by making them aware of the connection between their lost roots and their sickness. She *gave* them back confidence in their rituals, reconciled them with the ancestors, connected them again with tradition and could cure them in this way.

In the Townships around Cape Town, there are no specific sacrifice places and sacrifice rituals to contact the ancestors. However, sacrifices are

hereditary home country.

In the Townships we find in addition to the government structures with modern administration, hospitals, schools and police a second, traditional structure with kings, chiefs and healers.

At this second structure the major authority is represented by the traditional leaders who have created a hierarchy similar to the order in the former settlements. Any member of the community can turn to them with problems. They administer justice in cases of quarrels or violations of the unwritten rules of living together in the Townships. Their judgment is accepted by everyone. In cases of serious criminal offences the culprits are handed over to the police. The police are increasingly interested to co-operate with them. The government administration also tries hard to create closer connections to the traditional leaders and to use their influence on the population for the development of the community.

In Langa, the traditional leaders are united in an executive board. They form an umbrella under which the traditions are preserved. This board also supervises the activity of the "Sakhisizwe women", who are responsible for preparations and carrying out ceremonies according to old rites. They also produce the traditional clothing and the jewellery. Under this umbrella one also finds the group of the traditional healers. They are not only curing with herbs and traditional "medicine" but they keep the direct contact to the ancestors .

The shared identity, the common ancestors, traditions and rites celebrated together, give them the warmth and security of the known and familiar. This behaviour is found worldwide. The Germans living at the Cape have organized themselves in various associations and churches. They keep their traditions and roots. Old rituals such as Oktoberfest live on, and Christmas is celebrated as it was for centuries in wintry Germany in spite of midsummer temperatures. Another example is the Cameroonian Diaspora.. They founded an association in which the executive board is democratically elected. It takes great care of the members and has comprehensive authority.

If a member has problems like bereavement or illness in the family, or legal questions, he will get help and support. The president of this association is Abraham Njoya. He is also the grandson of the Sultan Ibrahim Njoya, king of the Bamum, one of the largest tribes of Cameroon. The king has selected Abraham Njoya to be the Chief, to be his representative and the supreme authority, and to have jurisdiction over the Bamooms in South Africa. His judgment is recognized respectfully by all Bamooms and all Cameroonians. He has a gallery for African art, and it is closed every Monday, for on this day he has his consulting hours and every Bamoom and Cameroonian can turn to him. There are many more examples of nations attempting to preserve their traditions and rites in order to retain the roots that support them far away from their

Top left: *Abraham Njoya, chief of the Bamum in S.A and his wife Jennifer*

Top right: *Sakhisizwe Cultural Women of Langa*

Below: *Prince Nosalchele Kote (left), and Prince P. Ngubenkosi Kote, speaker of the Langa chief*

Thoughts on the connection of religion and tradition

The lives of African people have always been infused by their ancestral religions which are an indispensable element in all areas of life. Culture, education, health, tradition - everything - is intertwined with the traditional religion.

The task of missionaries, the ambassadors of the new world, to make Christian belief accessible to the unbelieving African tribes was not too difficult. However, one commandment was never successfully transmitted : "You must have no other God but Me". Alongside the Christian God and parallel to this Creator, African people carry on honouring and worshipping their traditional gods and the spirits of the ancestors. In their daily lives they still have their tasks, and areas of responsibility pertaining to this earlier religion. Only Western European thinking sees a contradiction in going on Sunday morning for divine service and afterwards asking the traditional healer to contact the ancestors. This basis of intellectual and cultural life has hardly changed in Africa over centuries.

In Europe religion and secularity developed very differently. The separation between church and daily life grew greater and greater. Even the fact that the church over time created a hegemony of religion which was cemented in the period of witch-hunting, could not change this increasing separation. Over three centuries in Europe, 600,000 people (so- called witches) died, either burnt at the stake or during torture. The profession of the "witches" was practically eradicated throughout the continent. The "witches" of the past are what we call today in Africa the "traditional healers", "diviners", and "sangomas".

This professional group safeguards and preserves the traditions, and the net of connections between religion and daily life. It upholds the medical and spiritual wisdom of centuries. But this knowledge, this wealth, cannot be measured in terms of industrial growth and material prosperity and therefore it is often undervalued. Although the African people are so much richer in respect of their cultural heritage, the western world looks down on them and considers them behind the times. From the beginning of colonisation the African traditional religions were branded "the devil's evil" by the missionaries.

Today the countries of the "first world", whose prosperity is largely due to what they took from the colonies, is again attempting to influence Africa via aid to her developing countries, and to establish their own ideas of right and order, of good and evil. The war against terrorism further lowers Western tolerance towards other cultures, for being different seems threatening. It follows, therefore, that many visitors to African countries are themselves imprisoned by this narrow-mindedness.

∿∿Traditional Healers

In South Africa one can distinguish three groups of traditional African healers with different specialisations : *the traditional herbalist, the fortune teller and the witch doctor.*

A stranger looking for a Abakhulu Gogo will not easily find one. They have no company sign and do not advertise, yet people who need them know how to reach them. However,the herbalists, who are specialists in medicinal herbs, often have colourful sign-boards, and in order to attract the customers they present some of their products in front of their shops on the street. They are found all over the townships.

Esther Mbatha, an Abakhulu Gogo, is a *fortune teller.* Her history is unusual as she does not come from a rural region like most of her guild members, nor did she learn this profession from her parents. She is a genuine Capetonian. Her father, a black Portuguese, came from Maputo in Mozambique and her mother is a Xhosa woman from East London,. She was born in District Six and her mother tongue is Afrikaans. She grew up together with coloured and white children. When District Six was declared a white area, her family was moved with other black families to Guguletu. Resettlement was difficult since she spoke only Afrikaans and they now had to live in a Xhosa-speaking environment. However, they settled in and today she is still living here with her husband and her "baby", a twenty-one year old son. Two

other grown-up children have already got their own families.

Initially her life took a normal course, she had a job, she married, she had children. Then her father, whom she loved very much, died and his death plunged her into a deep depression. She was sick for a long time, virtually in the throes of death, and she recovered very slowly. After her convalescence, she suddenly noticed changes in herself and her environment. Dogs from the neighbourhood, though knowing her well, started growling at her and biting her. One day she saw her grandmother, who had been dead for a long time, sitting in front of her house on a bench. She asked her brothers if they could see her as well, but only she could see. That was her first direct contact with the ancestors.

Her two younger brothers left the house because they were frightened of their sister and thought she might be bewitched. Her older brother believed in her special abilities and advised her to train them. Esther herself felt sufficiently strong and willing to become an Abakhulu Gogo and she went to a famous school for traditional African healers in Gagankuku, near Swaziland. She had to leave her husband and her children for three years without ever contacting them. Training was held in several stages and the interpretation of dreams formed an important part of it. Every morning the pupils had to tell their own dreams in detail to the teacher and he interpreted them. In this way, the scholars were introduced to the secrets of dream interpretation. At the end of each training section, all pupils had to swim in a river which was teeming with crocodiles. Only those whose will was stronger than the will of the crocodiles passed the test.

The consecration as Abakhulu Gogo was celebrated with a three-day-long ceremony. The highlight of this event was the ritual sacrifice of two sheep. Esther had to place herself on the ground and a sheep was sacrificed on her body so that the blood of the animal poured over her body into earth. This established a direct connection between her and the ancestors, who then accepted her. This event took place in 1983, and since then she has been practising in Guguletu.

Before we visited Esther we had heard of her, but on arrival we were caught by surprise. There was no dim room filled with mystic objects

Main pic: *African pharmacy in Khayelitsha*
Top: *Fortune teller Esther Mbatha from Guguletu*
Above: *Shelves with herbs*

but a very inconspicuous, tiny house, where she lives together with her family. In the small living room which had a few pictures and much-used upholstered furniture, nothing indicated her unusual profession. But as soon as we met her, we felt that Esther was an exceptional woman, and we sensed the strength she radiated. After a short conversation we were asked to take our shoes off before following her into the next room, the bedroom of the house. In the narrow passage between bed and chest, we sat down cross-legged on the floor and face to face. Between us on a raffia mat was a chain, forming a ring. Esther shook and then opened a small container, and I had to blow into it three times before she closed it again, shook it once more and hit it three times on the ground. Then she opened the container to throw the contents into the ring on the floor, and my past and future was lying in front of me.

Top left: *Esther's house in Langa*
Left: *Esther Mbatha throws the bones*

Rae Graham describes in her book *White Woman Witchdoctor* how she interprets the bones: "*We look first at four wooden divining dice, which have a carved and a plain side, a head and a foot end. Limnana is the young woman; Twalima is the old woman; Tshilaumi is the young man; Lwahame is the old man. These four dice are the basis of our whole profession; you can divine with these only..... For six months you work with and learn about this basic family. Then comes the extended family, so you have to have a similar set made of something else. Then you go to the furthest extended family, and this is when you get the four ivory discs.*

Individuals will be singled out for specific readings, if necessary. There is a special medium-sized shell, a conch with a frilled edge, called the house of Amalozi (the house of the spirits), which is used in describing a person's house and the side of the entrance. A small white river pebble shows where the water source (the bathroom) is, and another one shows where the fire (kitchen) is. Most of the time the bones are right; you just have to learn to read them correctly. I cannot tell you why the patterns fall so accurately. That I cannot explain, and no one ever has described it to me. All I know is that most of the time the message is fully accurate, unless the reader is weak, out of practice, or has never properly learned the profession."

One of the best known herbalists in Cape Town is Major M. Ngolo from Langa. TV teams from the USA and Germany have reported on his pharmacy. It is a well- known and popular place for tour operators, and tourists come daily to meet an African herbalist. Major M Ngolo was born in the Keulani district in Transkei. He grew up with his grandparents who were also herbalists. As a child, his grandmother took him with her to collect herbs and explained to him the different healing effects. Later he was allowed to look over his grandfather's shoulder while he treated patients. He therefore grew up with this profession but did not really want to practise it. In 1981 he wanted adventure and, like many other young men, he set off for Cape Town as a contract worker. Here he found a job on the Railways. The Railways had big hostels in Langa where he lived for nine years, penned into a tiny room with other contract workers. Two to three times a year he went home to his grandparents and only then did he discover that he had a vocation for continuing the family tradition.

In 1990 he opened his own "African pharmacy" in Langa, the "Ndaba Herbal Chemist". Today he goes only occasionally to his home village to collect some specific herbs, but most of his basic raw materials he receives from suppliers country-wide. He has grown into a wholesaler, and many small herbalists from the region come and buy from him and compare notes.

Top: *The "African pharmacy" of Major M. Ngolo*
Above: *Herbalist Major M. Ngolo, Langa*

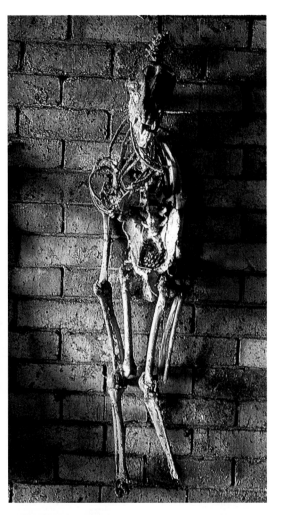

specific animal bones in a mortar. Somtimes he uses the powder, sometimes he mixes it with water or different oils. We spent some time looking around. From the ceiling hang strings with skins of snakes and other animals, parts of shark fins, bones, roots.... At the wall a skeleton of a baboon shows its teeth.When we ask why he needs all these things, he uses the example of a dried paw of a bushpig: "If a young mother comes to me because her baby is restless and howls too much, I take the baby in my arms, place the paw on his breast and say some very special sentences. Then I give the baby back to his mother and from now on it will be much calmer." If required, Major M. Ngolo also goes and visits the homes. His herbs do not only help cure illness, but other worries too. If the client is unlucky in busines, he uses a plant called Mbego, which he collects himself in the Transkei. At all four corners of the house, both inside and outside, he sets small bundles of the leaves alight. Thus the smoke does not only move through all the rooms but also covers the whole house : this, together with conjuring phrases, ejects the bad luck. And, it seems, by the next day the person's luck has turned. Of course, a person from a modern Western background would wonder whether the cause of this change lies in the herbs or the newly won self confidence.

Today the traditional healers are not only an integral part of traditional life,they find growing recognition in modern South African society. There is increasing cooperation between modern and traditional medicine.

photographs: *Everything, including animal skins is being used as medicine*

However, his main customers are still the usual people from Langa with their daily problems. Major M. Ngolo listens patiently to them and asks questions until he is sure of the cause of their problem or complaint so that he is able to prepare the right medicine. He makes all the medicines he prescribes himself. He crushes the dried ingredients like flowers, bark, roots or

Initiation

Once an old man explained initiation in this way: *"Children reaching the age of puberty are like freshly dried jackal skins which have to be tanned and cut to size, otherwise they become hard and useless. When we make bread, the flour, yeast and water have to be kneaded thoroughly, again and again. In the same way, during the phase of puberty the ingredients of life are brought together for our children. This takes place at the initiation school where they are kneaded thoroughly, again and again, so that the bread becomes crisp, fresh and good "*.

The training of the boys in the Xhosa initiation school, the "Vkwaluka", takes approximately five weeks. Only by passing tests does the boy become a real man, and accepted as a man by the other men and the whole Xhosa community. Vkwaluka forms one of the main pillars of Xhosa culture and is an indispensable component of social life. In the townships of Cape Town this ritual is performed according to traditional customs but has been adapted to city life. The date of the ritual is determined by the school holidays and the pupils do not have to walk into the distant mountains as is usual in the Eastern Cape. Instead, they go to a quiet open space near the townships.

Driving along the N2 during the time of initiation, one can see the round huts, the "ibhomas", in which the boys are living. They have been erected for this purpose on meadows beside the cooling towers of the Athlone power station.

Mvuzo Roy Dyasi and Alfred Yaya are members of the council of elders in Guguletu and they told us how they hold this ritual. When the boy is about eighteen years old, the parents decide on a date when their son will be ready for this school and when they will be able to afford the expense. They have to provide money for the fairly high charges of the teachers and of the man performing the circumcision, for the costs of the ceremonies, for three sacrificial animals (sheep or goats), for the food of the boy and his teacher during these five weeks.

Finally, they have to pay for a big final family celebration. In former times, the boys themselves earned the necessary money as contract workers in mines or factories. Today most of them are still at school and can hold only casual jobs in their leisure time or at weekends. Even these are difficult to find as there are many seeking jobs. The money earned is handed over to the father who manages it. Only when enough money has been saved can the father go to the council of elders and enrol his son to make sure that the rituals are carried out according to the rules . The members pass their experiences on to the teachers so that they can carry out the instruction and the examinations according to tradition.

The initiation begins with a ceremony when the first sacrificial animal will be slaughtered. All men of the family participate and receive some of the meat. The boy who is going for the Vkwaluka then leaves the house accompanied by his father and the male family members. At his arrival at the hut, the ibhoma, he has to take off everything he is wearing to show that he leaves his old life behind. For him a new period will start.

During this transitional period he is neither boy nor man and he is wrapped up only in an old blanket. He is not allowed to come into contact with his family and nobody except his teacher may touch him. He receives a stick, symbolizing a traditional hunting stick, which will be used to train him in stick fighting.

The initiate uses this stick instead of his hand for shaking hands. The little round huts are erected just for the initiates and are their home for the following five weeks. For each hut one teacher is appointed who will constantly look after his protégées and teach them. He paints the entire body of each initiate with white kaolin as a sign that they are now under the protection of the ancestors .

On the day of arrival, the ritual circumcision is carried out in the hut by a specially qualified member of the council of elders .

During the following seven days the teacher cares for the wound. This first week makes the highest demands on the initiates. The boys are in great pain, and to prevent bleeding they only get a few spoons of maize meal cooked in little water and nothing to drink at all. They are not allowed to leave the hut. Once a day the teacher renews the dressing of the wound and the white painting.

Previous page: *Teacher and scholar in the "Ibohma"*
Top left: *Afred Yaya and Mvuzo Roy Dyasi*
Left: *Ritual slaughtering of the sheep*
Above: *Preparation for the celebration meal*
Next page: *After seven days, the first real food*

During this time, they learn to bear pain, hunger and thirst, because this is what characterises a man and enables him to withstand the rigours of life. After the first seven days the second feast is celebrated, in which all male members of the community participate and the initiate may leave his hut and drink and eat. He has got over the worst of it. Now the second sheep is slaughtered, cut up and cooked in pots over the open fire. The first to eat is the initiate, and the tough meat is his first proper food for a week.

The banquet has started, the next to eat from the meat are the members of the council of elders and after that the younger ones may help themselves. During the cold winter time, hot soup is very popular. After the food the traditional African beer, Umgqombothi, is passed around in the same order as the meat before, but only the adult men drink, only they are allowed to consume alcohol. Only after completing their five weeks of apprenticeship, when the initiates are included in the world of the men, may they drink alcohol and have sex. During the four weeks which follow, the boys are taught by their teachers and they hear about their traditional customs, way of life and rituals. A very important part of their instruction is their learning of a secret language which is only spoken by men and used on special occasions. During the time of initiation the pupils are provided with food by their

families. Boys of the community regularly bring the food to them. Other visitors are an exception. Guests approaching this area have to announce themselves by a special long call, which is answered by the others. After completing the training, the father and the teacher of the initiate wash the white colour off the boy's body. Afterwards fat is rubbed on him in order to remove the last vestige and he receives a fresh blanket. His teacher presents a new hunting stick with knob to the initiate, a symbol that he is now capable and ready to stand his ground and defend his family. All items he has used during the last five weeks, his old blanket, his old stick, his shoes,

are burned together with the hut in which the boy became a man. He leaves his childhood and the time of crossing behind and returns home without looking back, accompanied by his father and the other male members of the family, wrapped up in a new blanket, with the new stick, as a man. He has to walk home. When he is within sight of his house, all women of his family and neighbourhood come towards him singing, cheering and with shouts of joy to accompany him on the last few metres of his way home. Here, all things of his childhood and of his past have been removed and new clothing is waiting forhim, to demonstrate the beginning of a new period of

his life. He is now a new person, a man. When he arrives home, the greatest party in the boy's life will be held, a feast in honour of the ancestors, who have admitted the young man into the ranks of adult men. A place of honour is prepared, marked out with fresh green twigs, and a mat

Top: *Initiates outside the "Vkwaluka"*
Top right: *After washing initiate is wrapped in a new blanket*
Middle right: *After completion of the initian school the "Vkwaluka" is set alight*
Below right: *The pupil has completed the initiation period and is taken home by the men*

is rolled out on which the pupil and his teacher take their place. The following celebration can last up to three days. It will be opened with speeches of the father and the master of ceremonies, who guides the course of the event, and of members of the council of elders. Umgqombothi is passed around. The ritual slaughtering of the third sheep follows. It starts with introducing the animal to the young man. He is told that his parents had to work very hard to make this whole procedure possible and that it he is expected from now on to make his contribution to the support of the family. The sheep is slaughtered by the eldest brother, who cuts the carotid artery with a knife. The blood of the sacrificial animal runs into a small pit in the sand, symbolizing that the cycle of life is completed. All life comes from the earth and the sap of life, the blood, is given back to the earth. The animal is skinned, gutted and cut up, the gallbladder is hung on a branch of a tree, to show that it can no longer spoil the meat. Beer and brandy circulate. The women, who are not allowed to be present during the sacrifice, are in the meantime celebrating exuberantly in the house. On the following day, there is the actual

celebration. The young man sits in his room with his closest friends, and his teacher assists him. Never ending streams of visitors come, often more than a hundred, with women in traditional Xhosa garments, their faces painted with stylised flowers. They bring presents and when handing them over, make little speeches which are accepted by the boy and his friends with heads reverently bowed.

All visitors are offered meat, potatoes and cooked corn and plenty of umgomboti is served. Every year at the time of the initiation ritual, in June and December, the debate on the continuance of these rituals is renewed in South Africa. Through the media one learns of boys who have died in the mountains of cold, hunger and thirst, of cases where the circumcision results in mutilation or HIV infection, of boys who die of injuries sustained during hard tests or punishments carried out by their teachers. Some initiation schools have been closed down on account of public protests, and there is a demand for government regulation and control. Nevertheless, most families decide to observe this ritual, and hope that the teacher is safe-guarding the life of their son, the life that is placed in his hands with such implicit trust.

Left page: *A delegation of men leads the initiates home*

Top: *Women of the community welcome the initiates with song and dance*

Above left: *The gallbladder on a tree*

Bottom left: *The master of ceremonies starts the celebrations*

Above right: *The first "Umgqombothi" in his life*

∿ funerals

The townships residents live here and now, hand to mouth. They surmount their present problems, and future problems will be solved in the future. Most of them have neither a medical-aid nor a pension scheme, and only in respect of their own funeral are provisions made. The funeral ceremony plays an important role in the social life of the township inhabitants. In order to ensure that this ceremony can be celebrated with dignity, they pay regularly into a funeral insurance scheme, although it is very difficult for them to raise the money even for this, and they have to borrow it and struggle to pay it back. The funeral ceremony follows strict rituals which depend partly on the financial situation of the family and the cause of the death. Many elements of this ceremony are ancient and passed on for generations, others have been adapted to life in modern cities.

When there is a death in the family, the dead person is laid out in a special room outside the house, the "mortuary", for one to two weeks. The family (who often arrive from all over the country for this special purpose) and the community now have an opportunity to say goodbye to the deceased. Throughout this time, a death-watch is kept, and family members, neighbours and friends pray beside the coffin. They are supplied

by the family with tea and traditional bread.

The funeral ceremony takes place on Saturdays and is organised by the family. On the Friday before the great celebration, cows or sheep are slaughtered for the feast. If the death was not from natural causes but was brought about by an accident or a crime, no animals are slaughtered, because they believe that then further family members will be stricken by death. In these cases, they buy animals already slaughtered, mostly chickens. Often a huge tent is erected for the many mourning guests. On the day of the burial, the coffin, now closed and decorated with flowers, is placed in front of the home. The family, the neighbours and the closest friends arrive in the early morning. No invitations are sent, for everybody knows, and appearance is taken for granted. Those present receive a printed programme. The priest of the parish opens the ceremony. He speaks about the deceased, his career, his position in society and in the family.

We visited a remembrance ceremony, held by Reverend Mr Mkhete in honour and memory of forty-three year- old Christa Moyake. She had become a victim of a family tragedy. After twenty years of marriage, she wanted to leave her husband. He could not bear this and fatally shot his wife first and then himself. The deceased was a teacher and she was very popular so more than three hundred guests came to her funeral. During his speech the minister urges all those present to have charity. Afterwards, the coffin is brought in a hearse to the church where the dead woman had been a member, St. Anthony's Catholic Church. Every seat is filled and the priest celebrates the requiem. Starting from this place, the last escort is given to the dead woman, and a big convoy consisting of more than forty cars and minibuses and four coaches accompanies the coffin to the cemetery.

At the grave the priest says a last prayer and sprays the coffin with holy water before it is

Left page: *Reverend Mkhete honours the dead and cautions the living,*

Top: *Inside Catholic Church, Langa*

Bottom: *At the cemetary*

lowered. The women are singing and the song goes straight to one's heart. This is their way of saying goodbye. The men of the family and community close the grave, the women throw a last handful of earth on it.

In the meantime neighbours and friends have prepared the food for the guests in the home of the deceased. In front of the house are bowls of water and soap, where the members of the family wash their hands and then the guests do likewise. With this symbolic action, the death is washed off their hands. Cooked maize kernels are then passed around, for they believe that eating the maize kernels also keeps away death .Then the funeral reception begins, with catering for all several hundred of the guests. As in all celebrations, men and women eat separately. The family members who sit down in the house, the women in the living-room, the men in the kitchen, are served first and there are no alcoholic drinks.This communal meal brings the first part of the funeral solemnity to an end. After this begins the second part of the ceremony, called "after tears". The last feast takes place for the dead. All guests, all friends and members of the family go to a party room, not far away for a social get-together with plenty of *umgqombothi*, music and dance. This is the last time the deceased is together with friends and relatives in a spiritual sense. She is honoured and can now enter the world of the ancestors. There she can act on behalf of her surviving dependants.

Above: *Washing hands after the funeral*

Top right: *Final goodbye at the gravesite*

Middle right: *Offering the cooked maize kernals*

Bottom right: *Women sitting in the living room*

Next Page: *Neighbours and friends dishing out the food for three hundred guests*

Social adversities
and Self-help projects

you want to build a ship, don't drum up the men to gather
od, divide the work and give orders.
tead, teach them to yearn for the vast and endless sea.
for the future, your task is not to foresee it, but to enable it

Antoine de Saint-Exupéry

~~~ Social Problems

A survey carried out in 1999 among the inhabitants of Khayelitsha specified the following problems, in order of significance: Unemployment 70;Alcohol abuse 30; Illiteracy 29; Teenage pregnancies 19; Tuberculosis 19; Drug abuse 18; Violence in the family 17; Child abuse15; AIDS14; Gangs and crime 13

This assessment is subjective, as most social workers and other experts regard unemployment, crime and AIDS as the main problems.

In 2001 the unemployment rate in South Africa was about 30% . In the Townships of Cape Town 50% to 70% of the population are estimated to be unemployed. There is no safety net of social benefits and so the unemployment causes severe social problems like poverty and criminality. Many jobless people try to earn some money as casual workers.

Driving through the suburbs of Cape Town in the morning, one sees men waiting at certain crossroads. They are hoping for a job -from building contractors who will pass, looking for some helpers for the day - from people needing a casual labourer for the garden or other hard work. Many of them will be unlucky. They will lay out money for a bus-ticket and then wait in vain for many hours. Others attempt to keep their head above water as hawkers, selling fruit, vegetables and basic commodities on the street. The most depressing way of looking for work is going from house to house in order to ask for some kind of employment.

The South African Police reported in September 2001 that the crime rate had decreased in South Africa for the first time in recent years.

This progress was seen as an initial success in

Left: *Unemployed family begging*
Top: *Bussiness on wheels*
Bottom: *Casual labourers waiting for jobs*

the government programme for fighting crime although the statistics are still very high compared to international standards.

Cape Town, however, is one of the more secure cities in South Africa. Yet if you talk to township dwellers on the topic of crime, everyone has a story about being a victim of crime. Burglary, theft, robbery are not unusual. It often hits those who are even poorer than the criminals because they are weaker and can hardly protect themselves.

The police are chronically understaffed and many crimes are not even reported because the victims don't have any confidence in the ability of the police to solve them.

Unemployment

He wakes up early in the morning
to look for a job
But not much is in store for him
And he asks why this happens to him
He goes out to buy a newspaper
And he sees a job, so he phones
Sorry the job has been filled
He went out to go door to door
But still there's no luck.

When he enters the premises
The big "No Vacancy" sign greets him
But he ignores it and goes right in
A big lady at the reception,
Without even looking at him says
"There is no vacancy".

He goes home deflated
His stomach is so empty
Because he was not filled
This morning and yesterday
Why is this world so cruel.

He searches his pocket to buy something
But the remaining money is for the return home
As a man, he must presevere
Because this world is not for men
But it is a living reality.

by Mike Nduna
Reprinted with friendly permission of Eric Klaas Comunications cc

AIDS, one of South Africa's main concerns, was only in ninth place in the response people made about their social problems in 1999. That indicates the enormous need for education. To meet this need, the government launched an information and education programme as part of a comprehensive strategy to fight AIDS. This campaign will be intensified within the next years. AIDS has become an important topic in schools, there are informative posters in public institutions and hospitals, condoms are distributed free of charge.

Statistics prove the alarming dimensions of the epidemic. The depressing report of a teacher from a township school in Philippi shows the impact of this situation on daily life, for in her class eight pupils have already lost mothers owing to Aids.

Moreen, a mother in Lwandle, has nine children, five of whom have left home and are self-supporting. She has adopted parentless children into her family for years and is now caring for fourteen children in addition to her own. Soon she will take four more children under her wing whose mothers have recently died of Aids. Nine of the children she looks after are HIV positive. She carries her "baby" on the arm, a three year-old boy, suffering from AIDS. He can neither see nor speak, and she has become very attached to this helpless orphan. To provide for her big family, she depends on donations from the church, and is looking forward to receiving a washing machine soon. The government makes great efforts to solve these problems but the possibilities are limited.

The township people are dependent on the aid of NGO's (non- governmental organizations) like churches, and charity organizations. These NGO's and many inhabitants of the townships themselves, have launched numerous auxiliary projects which are dealing with the main problems of unemployment, crime and AIDS. Although much has been achieved, a tremendous amount still needs to be done.

Top: *Aids information campaign in Khayelitsha.*

Right: *Moreen and "her baby" from Lwandle.*

Independent Chris Hani School Langa

In 1991 the inhabitants of the Joe Slovo Squatter camp, together with some teachers and Maureen Jacobs, the present principal, joined forces to found the Independent Chris Hani School, Langa.

This school takes children who came with their parents from the former Homelands and have settled in the Joe Slovo Squatter camp. Many of the children have no documents like birth certificates, which are required to attend a government school. The Independent Chris Hani School looks after these children. It does not see its task as only bringing them up to the required level of education, but also as supplying them with school reports and introducing them to expected urban social behavior. The children learn how to use traffic lights, telephones and escalators and how to behave in the new setting of the squatter camp, where people live together in cramped surroundings. This is often very difficult for children who are used to life in the sparsely populated countryside.

The demand for places in this school is almost insatiable. However, shortage of money limits the growth of the school. It finances itself only to a limited degree by school fees, which are R20 per

month, and many parents are not able to scrape even this amount together. The government subsidy is very small and irregular. The main source of income are the tourists who visit the school daily during their township tours and are received with enthusiasm.

Maureen takes the visitors through the class rooms and explains to them the problems and the aims of this type of schooling. At the end of the

This is a Lions project of the **LC Tokai** and the **LC Agenda 21 Dresden** / Germany
Sponsored by:
Birkart International, Galerie Sillack, Kalahari

isit, the children sing some songs. The mainly oreign tourists are strongly impressed by the xcellent spirit of the teachers and children, who re working with few material resources in poor urroundings, but with a lot of pride. No wonder, hen, that most visitors feel they wish to give a onation to this school and nobody passes the ollecting box at the exit without contributing. oth parties gain during these visits. The visitors et to know something about the real life nd work at a township school and the school an improve its finances.

Even so, the school account allows only a very neager teacher salary of R500.00 per month (in ;ood months R1000.00). Nevertheless, all 10 eachers work with great enthusiasm. They are roud to have enabled thousands of children to nter government schools over the years and to ave spared them the destiny of becoming street hildren like so many others.

During the first six months of 2002, the school was able to extend its capacity from 315 children to 580. The money for this was raised in a joint project of the Lions Clubs Tokai in Cape Town and Agenda 21 in Dresden, Germany.

These two clubs organized an art exhibition in Dresden in 2001, gathering more than 150 artworks of 8 artists from the Cape area under the title "Art of the Rainbow Nation". A children's drawing competition between the Chris Hani School, the German School Cape Town and the Oberschule Dresden was organized to run parallel to this. All the children's art works, emerging from this competition were shown at the big exhibition and 12 pictures were used to print a calendar.

All net profits benefited the Chris Hani School. Two new classrooms were built, furnished and equipped with teaching materials, so that more than 200 additional children could be admitted.

Above: *The first grade with 90 pupils in their windowless classroom*

Bottom: *Opening of the two new classrooms through the german vice council Rainer J. Theisen*

Left page top : *Maureen the principal with choir from the Chris Hani School*

Left page bottom: *The two new classrooms were sponsored by Lion's International*

ᔕᔕᔕ Learn to Earn

Learn to Earn is a very professionally led project of the Baptist church which was launched in 1989 by Douglas and Yvonne Fisher. The aim is to provide unemployed people with the knowledge of special crafts in training courses, and to enable them to start up their own businesses. Courses are offered for sewing, baking, weaving, business basics and computer training for desktop publishing. But it is not only a question of imparting knowledge, it is an attempt to familiarise the participants with the philosophy of the project, *"A Hand Up, Not a Hand Out"*. The results of the last twelve years are remarkable. More than 5000 people, in most cases unemployed township citizens, have completed training successfully. Many of them proceeded into self employment, and have even employed other workers themselves.

Douglas, who lived in the USA for a long time, knew how to make contacts, both overseas and in South Africa. The list of the local sponsors,who are financing 60% of the budget, reads like a Who's Who of South Africa.

There are big insurance companies, famous supermarket chains and cigarette companies,

esigner boutiques, hotel associations, sport lubs, churches and private people supporting he project. The remaining 40% of the budget s donated by the USA, particularly by churches. n 2000 they were able to move to a new, very eautiful building in Khayelitsha, built by articipants of their courses. These formerly nemployed people were trained in the rogramme as construction workers. The interior ttings were also made in their own workshops. Now the twenty instructors, the manager and the litha Parking Community Church, founded *Learn o Earn*, can work under one roof.

Wilfred Reynolds used to be a farmer. Convinced by the idea of the project, he sold his arm and is now its head of the Department of Communication and Public Relations, not a very vell paid post.

The coffee bar "The Odd Cup", also a part of he project, opened in 2001. Products of its own vorkshops are exhibited and for sale, with tourists n mind. Once a month, a business breakfast takes lace in the cafe. Wilfred explains:" We want to reate a bridge between the rich southern suburbs f Cape Town and the townships, and this reakfast is a way to make the project accessible o businessmen. We have already won many ponsors in this way." With a friendly smile Nobom Ntsuntsane serves a gigantic muffin, fresh rom the baking course, with butter and jam and ot coffee, "bottomless", as much as one wants, or only 10 Rand.

The basic tailoring course ends today and the articipants are practising songs and dances ecause the end of the course will be celebrated his evening. In an following advanced training ourse, they will make use of their skills and roaden them at industrial sewing machines. There is a similar situation in the joinery, where in a five-week course basic carpentry is taught vith hand tools. After this course, a ten week dvanced training is offered, and during this raining one works on wood- processing nachines. As a finale, everyone has to construct table, chair or cupboard. For every course, onsisting of handicraft and management parts, he participants have to pay 120 Rand. This covers only a fraction of the costs of 4500 Rand per rainee. The fee mainly represents a symbolic ontribution, as a course free of charge would not e accepted as valuable, Wilfred said. The next mbitious target of Learn to Earn is the stablishment of a business centre, where good opportunities should be created for trainees who lan to start up their own business. Further rojects could be initiated by other churches ollowing this model. In addition to the main

institution in Khayelitsha, there are now branches of Learn to Earn in Durbanville and Hermanus.

Top left page: *Display of products manufactured by the project*

Bottom left page: *Inside the "Coffee Bar"*

Above top: *Desktop publishing course*

Middle: The *joinery workshop*

Bottom: *Service with a smile*

Waldorf School in Philippi & Khayelitsha

On the German home page of " Freunde der Erziehungskunst Rudolf Steiner e.V" we can read the following: "Waldorf Education for 6000 township children in South Africa: When a small Waldorf School in Philippi, a township near Cape Town (South Africa) opened its gates at the beginning of 1999,one hundred children were expected but one hundred and fifty children came to be admitted. With great effort, the parents of the children raised money and built a further wooden classroom. In addition to the second class, two first classes were then created."

We wanted to present this joint venture between the school in Philippi and the German Waldorf Association as a example of a successful international project and so we visited the Waldorf School in Philippi. But we found that the school had been closed, and the buildings stand empty and dilapidated. Only the separate kindergarten is still running. The head of the kindergarten, Nombalero Majezi, told of her experiences. In 1994 she founded the kindergarten with 15 children from Philippi. Later, she came into contact with the Waldorf School in Cape Town, which made it possible for her to take part in a three- year teacher- training course. Between the Philippi kindergarten and the Waldorf Centre for Creative Education in Cape Town a close collaboration began.

In 1999, a Waldorf School was opened in Philippi, a centre of hope for the inhabitants of this region. In 2001 the school was suddenly closed when the financial support by the government was withdrawn and the parents were not able to pay school fees which covered running costs. Since then, Nombalero Majezi again fights alone for the survival of the kindergarten, where she cares for one hundred and forty children. From the community she receives monthly 6600 Rand each month, which has to cover all costs, including food. Donations from the church and visitors to the institution, help with the financial problems. Nombalero, now a convinced Waldorf pedagogue, feels herself let down. However, she still has hopes that one day the urgently required school will be opened again. After inquiring in Germany, we were informed that the school had to be closed through lack of parental commitment. We were

old that a Waldorf School has to be financed partly by the parents: because that had not been possible, the school had ceased to exist.

In Philippi, where the poorest of the poor are living, it is impossible. The answer to my letter to Germany closes with these words: "We have come to the sober conclusion that many initiatives, once they are detached from the white helpers, do not bloom anymore."

There is great disappointment on both sides. Nombalero feels herself let down and misunderstood and the people in Germany get the impression that their help was not accepted, that the project was not continued in the spirit of its inception.

Other Waldorf projects in the Townships Cape Town are successful. So the Zenzeleni School work independently) which was founded in January 1995 in Khayelitsha by parents and the Centre for Creative Education", an institute for Waldorf education. They started with one class . Three years later there were already classes up to grade fifth and the school expands every year. So the pupils who started with grade one will be able to complete their school training here. The school budget is financed with two thirds by the Waldorf institute and one third by the parents. They often have to struggle to raise the money although they don't belong to the poorest ones,

they don't live in the squatter camps. The school is managed to a great extent by a parents board. The board members make decisions concerning the budget and the steps which have to be take against parents who failed to pay the school fees. So the term of payment may be extended or even waived partially in cases of a temporary economic plight. Thanks to the support by the Centre for Creative Education the Zenzeleni School has a comparatively high level of material and staff equipment.

Visitors are always welcome, the achievements are shown with pride and optimism.

Left page:
Nombalero and the Waldorf Kindergarten in Philippi

Above: *Grade 5 classroom in the Zenzeleni school in Khayelitsha*

Left: *Grade 4 classroom in Zenzeleni school*

ᴧᴧᴧ Everyone can learn

In 2000, two social workers in Langa, Mpumi Ngoqo and Nosipho Sikutshwa teamed up and started the project Everyone Can Learn. It comprises two programmes. The first one enables township citizens to make use of the available ground in order to plant vegetables, fruit and flowers for their own consumption or to sell in the community.

The second program deals with the training of women in different practical courses in order toenable them to start up their own businesses, andto become self-supporting. In many courses the participants receive management training as well. This equips the women to run their small businesses efficiently. Several training programmes have successfully given courses in market gardening where the graduates were shown how to produce vegetables and fruit for their own use and for sale. Since government subsidies for projects of this kind are very small and no sponsors have been found, finance is a permanent problem. The community made the premises available to the project but there is no money for equipping the training rooms and the office, or for training

materials or for teachers. But nevertheless some positive results have been achieved during the last two years. The two founders of the project have grown close to the community and enjoy their full confidence, so there are many voluntary helpers,contributing to particular projects without payment. One volunteer is Douglas Mkhosi, grandfather of a pupil, who works every day for several hours without payment in a school garden project of *Everyone Can Learn*.

The school garden is part of a project carried out in collaboration with the Imbasa Primary School in Cross Roads. Two years ago Mpumi and Nosipho, together with three teachers of this school, launched a gardening and environmental group. It is an attempt to awaken environmental awareness in children in a very simple way. For instance, pupils have to clean the schoolyard and buildings themselves, so they are careful not to drop any litter.

In the newly introduced subject of Nature Study, the children receive basic information which can be of good use in the school garden. They are very involved in their gardening and they tend and observe their plants from the seed to the fruit. The head of the group, the teacher of class 3, tells us that in cooperation with the parents and the community, they have also been able to reduce violence and crime at the school. The greatest problem now is the high unemployment amongst

parents, two thirds of whom are without a job and cannot afford the low school fees. A growing HIV-AIDS infection rate plunges families deeper and deeper into poverty. Eight mothers died of Aids in one class alone. The affected children are looked after by relatives, mostly by their grandparents, who are often not able to care for them adequately.

Left: *Pupil of the "Imbasa Public Primary" school proudly showing off the fruits of his labour*

Top: *Pupils of the "Imbasa Public Primary" school*

Bottom: *Mpumi and Nosipho, the founders of "Every one can learn" in their Langa office*

Pupils come to school hungry and badly prepared. However, the vegetables harvested by the school's garden group are used in the school kitchen to satisfy the children's hunger.

There are plans to fence in available, unused ground and to cultivate it as part of the project *Everyone Can Learn*. This will be done by the parents of the children, and will contribute to their personal needs and improved living.

There is a further project still in its infancy, offering training in market-gardening to other unemployed people. The target is the Langa Day Hospital where about 30 tuberculosis patients daily receive their medication under professional supervision. Since highly nutritive food is an important aspect of therapy and since this is often not guaranteed at home, the patients receive warm soup in addition to the medicine.

The hospital has funds only for the pharmacological treatment, but the soup is prepared in the hospital kitchen from donated food, At the moment, this food is delivered on aweekly basis by the Lions Club as part of the Lions Food Project.

The *Everyone Can Learn* project is to lay out a vegetable garden on grounds provided by the hospital. Here the TB patients will work for one or two hours a day after they have received their medication and their meal under the guidance of a voluntary worker. Market gardening, with active input of the people who will benefit, should produce enough vegetables to enable the day hospital to cover its own needs. More ground is available so that an extension of the vegetable garden is planned for the future, and any surplus can be sold.

Such work also has a positive side effect, for the often unemployed, depressive patients now have a duty and therefore feel needed and a useful part of society again.

At the moment the vegetables are insufficient for their own kitchen where Madlamini daily prepares the meals for the patients. There is clearly still a long way to go before marketing the vegetables.

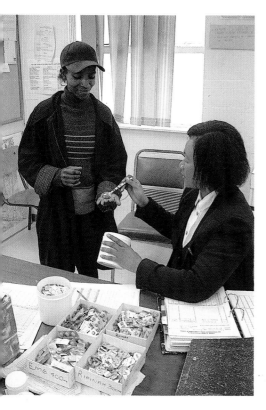

Another project is the home-bakery of Erica Jardine. One and a half years ago Erica started up her own business with the support of the project *everyone Can Learn*. Her freshly baked doughnuts are especially popular at nearby schools. She receives orders for wedding- or birthday-cakes whichshe creates in her little kitchen. She and her family can make a living off the net profit of the bakery.

Now Erika would like to pass on her collected experiences to other women. For this purpose, a training course in the *Everyone Can Learn* centre is planned for 10 women. Here they will get business training for their self employment. Erica will also give lessons on professional baking in a four-week course. The expected snowball effect should have a positive influence on the entire community.

Top left page: *Douglas Mkhosi, grandfather of one of the pupils is in charge of the gardening project*

Bottom left page: *T.B patients enjoying their cup of soup*

Left: *Patient recieving her daily treatment*

Right: *Erica Jardine in her bakery*

Chris Hani Indepent School
Joe Slovo Squatter camp, Langa 7455
Tel: 021 6952441/Cell: 0721252511
Principal: Maureen Jacobs

Every One Can Learn
Nr 21 Cnr Mama & Ndlwana Ways
Settler's Place
Langa 7455
Tel: 021 6955864/Cell: 0836908977
Contact: Mpumi Ngoqo

Learn to Earn
Sixwayikati
Khayelitsha
Tel: 021 3615972
Contact: Wilfred Reynolds

Zenzeleni School for Creative Education
64 Mongesi Rd.
Khayelitsha
Tel: 021 3610613
E-mail: zenzeleni@cfce.org.za

Tourism and Business life

...e key seems to be to let your actions express you and work to
...e everything you express something you are proud of.

Marlo Morgan, Message From *Forever*

~~~ Tourism in the Townships

Over the last few years, great efforts have been made to put the Townships of Cape Town on the map, and to make them one of the attractions for the growing number of tourists who come to South Africa. With the support of the City of Cape Town and the Community based Development Fund a considerable tourist infrastructure has been developed, with projects like the Outlook Platform and the Tourist Information in Khayelitsha, the Tourist Information in Guguletu and the Migrant Labour Museum in Lwandle. The increasing interest of the tourists not only in the city centre of Cape Town and the rich suburbs but also in the townships around Cape

Town brings more and more visitors. This stimulates the private initiatives of many township inhabitants and B&B's, restaurants, craftsmen and travel organisers have established themselves. Compared to the big tourist projects of Cape Town this is very modest, but it is a start and makes the townships more attractive for tourism. It points the way to future development for these places. Unfortunately, any person who would like to explore the townships on his own initiative doesn't get too much information in the central Tourist Information in Cape Town. At least he will hear about the Sivuyile (Our Luck) Tourist Centre in Guguletu. This is a valuable hint, and it is easy to

Left page: *Lookout Hill in Khayelitsha*
Top: *Flody (left) the manageress of the Sivuyile Tourist Centre*
Other pics: *Inside the Sivuyile Tourist Centre*

find with the help of a map and the little pamphlet provided. Arriving at this place, one discovers a real goldmine of information and tips. The team working here is not only very friendly and helpful, they also have sound knowledge. On request one receives lists with information on B&B's, restaurants, cafes or artists. An exhibition, prepared with loving care, of informative posters telling the history of Guguletu and a worthwhile sales exhibition of the local artists make the Sivuyele centre a tourist magnet. A further Information Centre is in Khayelitsha, in the big **Oliver Tambo Sports Centre**. Here one can receive many valuable tips, pamphlets and brochures. If you would like to go to the townships with a guide you can book for one of the numerous available tours, and information is available at Cape Town's Tourist Information. "Khwela-Khwela" (come purely) has been offering these excursions for some time. Since 1993, Mr P. Gumenche has been taking tourists through the townships. Because of the increasing demand, his company has expanded and he now owns four mini buses, and he also offers, in addition to the usual half day tours, Shebeen Tours" (pub tours) on Fridays and "Church Tours" on Sundays.

Faizal Gangal guides township tours for Cape Capers Tours. It is very important to him

that his visitors are really in touch with township life, not just pass through in closed buses.

Therefore, he takes extensive walks with his guests through Langa, and introduces them to the herbalist or his friends and acquaintancs in the market. We met Faizal in the Guga s'Thebe Centre in Langa and since his tourists were occupied at the craft market, he had time to tell us a little story:

Above: *Tourist on township tour*

Left page: *Traditional healers from Langa in front of the Guga's Thebe*

Below: *Tourists visiting the Chris Hani School in Langa*

Some weeks ago I went through Woodstock, a region where there are normally no tourists. I saw two women standing on the pavement. They were German visitors who had made a Township tour with me the day before. I stopped and asked them whether I could help. They told me that they had been very deeply impressed by the tour through the townships. The visit to a tiny shack, where a family of five was living, had given them a sleepless night. During breakfast they spontaneously decided to help this family, and to buy beds, pillows and bedding for them. I invited the ladies into my bus, they went shopping and spent R20,000 and we took everything to the family who were of course extremely grateful. Yes, Faizal finished his story, *tourists often do the unexpected.*

Mpumi Nogu gladly guides visitors through Langa, Nyanga and Guguletu. As head of the project "Everyone can Learn" she especially enjoys showing her projects. For many years she used to be a social worker in Langa, now she is known everywhere and anyone who goes with her will be impressed not only by her great knowledge but also by her warmth. There is a place in her heart for everybody. She also knows most of the shebeens and on request she takes her visitors there, where you can have a beer and come into contact with the residents.

A visitor who prefers a German-speaking guide will be in good hands with Michael Telschow, author of this book. He runs a small guesthouse **"Africa Connection"** and he is a recognized township specialist, responding to the individual wishes of his visitors.

Above: *Children with tourist bus in Langa*

Right: *Monwabisi Maqugi, the tour guide from Khayelitsha and his family*

Tygerberg Tourism
(Khayelitsha Info Centre)
Oliver Tambo Centre
Lansdowne Road / Mew Way
Khayelitsha 7784
Tel/Fax: 021 364 9660

Sivuyile Tourism Centre
corner NY 1 & NY 4
Guguletu 7750
Tel: 021 637 8449
E-mail: Guguletu@mweb.co.za
www.sivuyile.co.za

Khayelitsha Lookout Tower
corner M44 Mew way & M32 Spine Rd

Township tour operators: page 131

My name is Monwabisi Maqogi. I was born in 1967 in Queenstown and now I live in Cape Town, South Africa.

I was an active member of the African National Congress in the 1980's and worked as part of the underground, fighting against the apartheid government. I was severely tortured and imprisoned on four occasions. In 1985 I was detained under the state of emergency, taken to the police station and tortured. This involved being electrocuted. And having a money bag with water put over my head with electric wire on my ears. On another occasion, they put a tyre around my neck, placed my hands behind my back and threw matches at my hair. They made me lie down and kicked me, suffocated me and crushed my private parts. I thought I was going to die.

One time I was tortured over a five day period and then taken to Worcester, a town not far from Cape Town. I was later detained under section 29, the legal provision that allowed extended detention without charges for six months during which time I was further tortured. In 1988 I underwent a trial in Worcester and was sentenced to six years imprisonment.

I was released in 1992. I have been emotionally scarred from what I have had to endure. I have been in counselling. I have sacrificed a huge amount as part of the struggle to end apartheid in South Africa. The lack of both recognition of my role in the struggle and financial support leaves me with additional pain. I have a wife and two children, son and daughter, but I am unable to work. I'm trying to do the tourism that will provide me and my family. The tourism is called Themalethu Tourism (our hope).

In my tours I tell the tourist's about my history, the past African history and the Truth Commission, and about the history of black townships. They must communicate with the people in our area, and that they must feel free, welcomed in the spirit of Ubuntu (togetherness). There after I take them to a restaurant called Igugu Le Africa to to have something to eat.

This is my life story.

Those who do not want to be in a group but want a guide for a private tour, should look for **Monwabisi Maqugi**. He shows the townships to his visitors, using their cars, under the motto: "I show you the past". He was active in the struggle for freedom : he knows all the corners and places and has a story to tell about the fight against apartheid for each of them. It is important for him that his visitors get the "township feeling". He doesn't keep an eye on the time when he is out with tourists.

For him a tour is finished when he knows that his visitors are satisfied, and he has shown and told them all that is necessary to give them an impression of life in the township. After a tour, he loves to invite his guests to his new house, his pride, which he was able to build with the financial assistance of an American Baptist Church.

Monwabisi Maqogi:
BB 126 Town 12 Khayalitsha, Cape Town,
Cell: 083 518 4508

Africa Connection:
P. O Box 2534, Clareinch 7740
Tel: 021 683 6611/ Fax: 021 683 1087
E-mail: Michaelt@uninetwork.co.za

Mpumi Ngoqo:
21 Cnr Mama & Ndlwana Ways
Settler's Place Langa 7455
Cell: 083 690 8977

Malebo's- Khayelitsha

Lydia Masoleng has run this small guesthouse with her daughter for three years. It is very close to public transport because it is near the major Walter Sisulu Road. She can accommodate visitors in three double rooms. She offers such good service that she has won prizes in guesthouse competitions. The price for the overnight stay includes a walk through the residential area. She also offers different tours through the townships. The shebeen tour is very popular as there are visits to several shebeens on its itinerary and the guests can get into conversation with many people. She also knows all the craftsmen and women in her Township and gladly leads her visitors to them, for one can get good value for money. In addition to B&B, she also offers dinner for her guests. She then prepares Xhosa food, Mugyusha, a dish from beans and corn, and serves it together with her self-brewed *Umgomboti*. If there are too many guests booking for dinner, she confidently recommends her cousin. He runs the restaurant "Igulu et Africa", which is only 10 minutes walk from her guesthouse. She has already had B&B guests from the USA, Holland, the UK and other countries. Everybody who goes through Khayelitsha with Lydia develops a special affinity to this lively, hustling, bustling township and will think back affectionately to this stay. Some of her visitors become friends and they keep in regular correspondence.

Malebo's Bed and Breakfast
Lydia Masoleng
18 Mississippi Way, Grace Land,
Khayelitsha, 7784
Tel: 021 361 2391 Cell: 083 475 1125

For Frederic, the French student we disturbed during his breakfast, she had arranged a visit to the Joe Slovo Primary School, and he is still strongly impressed by that visit. Frederic had completed several months of practical training at a distinguished winery before he crowned his stay in South Africa with a journey around the country. In a few days he has to go back to France, and leaving is difficult for him. "Only with Thobe, have I learned something different of South Africa and the realities of the black majority of the population," he says.

Thobe has good reason to be proud of her kitchen, too. She loves to prepare traditional Xhosa food and makes ginger ale for her visitors.

Kopanong- Khayelitsha

Kopanong - where the world meets. And really, the list of visitors is international. Thope Lekan has B&B guests from many countries, from Europe, America and Australia. She is particularly proud that the British Secretary of State stayed with her. Some weeks ago a married couple with two small children from Cape Town spent a weekend with her. The parents wanted to make the township life familiar to their children and, indeed, they played all the time with the neighbourhood children. Thope has run her little guesthouse since 1999.

In 2002, she added a further room so that she now has three guest rooms available. With the ingenious furnishings, crockery and bed and table linen she creates an African flair in her house. Thope is a veteran of the anti-apartheid fight but when you meet this friendly, lively woman and talk to her, you do not get the impression that there is a fighter in front of you. In the nineties she worked as a development worker for rural areas. Then she took a three year training course to became a certificated and approved tour guide of the government tourism organization Satour. She doesn't want to offer only B&B to her visitors but also professional service. Together with her, one can undertake tours through the townships and come into contact with the residents.

Kopanong B & B- Thope Lekau
Tel & Fax: 021 361 2084
Cell: 082 476 1278
E- mail:Kopanong@xsinet.co.za
C329 Velani Crescent, Khayelitsha 7784
PO Box 22, Khayelitsha 7783
Cape Town, South Africa

Ma Neo's B&B

The name Ma Neo is made up of Ma for mama and Neo, the name of her daughter. Zodema, who runs the guesthouse, used to be a nurse with all her heart and soul. A chronic asthma condition forced her into early retirement. One morning she heard on the radio about B&B's in Khayelitsha and she felt that this was precisely the right thing for her. She called the guesthouse in Khayelitsha in order to get some inside information and to learn form their experiences. There she received the important advice to take a relevant course, and this she did.

She used all her savings and the severance pay she received from the hospital and built an extension of three double rooms and bathrooms according to her own plans. Although she is situated in a good area in Langa, quite near to the city, it was not easy to begin with, but she survived. During this time her daughter was a big help, for she gave her a computer and showed her how to use it. By now, Zodema has accommodated visitors from many countries who appreciate her outstanding cooking which is well known all over Langa. With her guests, she goes for walks through Langa, meeting the herbalist Major M. Nydo, who is right around the corner, or to visit the taverns which are within easy walking distance. On request she also fetches her visitors from the airport - perfect service.

Ma Neo's B & B
No 30 Zone 7, Langa 7745
Cape Town
Ph. 021 694 2504
cell. 073 146 0370
or Zodwa@ 072 158 6921

Luyola Guesthouse

Pincky Majikela also started a guest house which she calls "Luyola"(Joy). She saw a television programme about guest houses in Gauteng. That gave her the idea and in 1999 she opened the first B&B in Guguletu. Looking at Pincky one can see the "joy" for she is always cheerful and laughs and this spreads to her visitors. During the summer season the four double rooms are often fully booked, though it is quieter in winter.

Nobody knows Guguletu as well as Pincky does and she proudly shows her township to the visitors. Her cooking is very popular, as she combines traditional Xhosa food with western cuisine. The cosy living-room is a meeting place for everybody and the visitors often sit until late and talk to their hostess. Most of the guests come from South Africa but visitors from Germany and other countries in Europe have also enjoyed the hospitality and the pleasant personality of Pincky.

Luyola Guesthouse
24 Dabula Crescent
Luyoloville, 7750
Tel: 021 934 7299
Cell: 082 849 9332

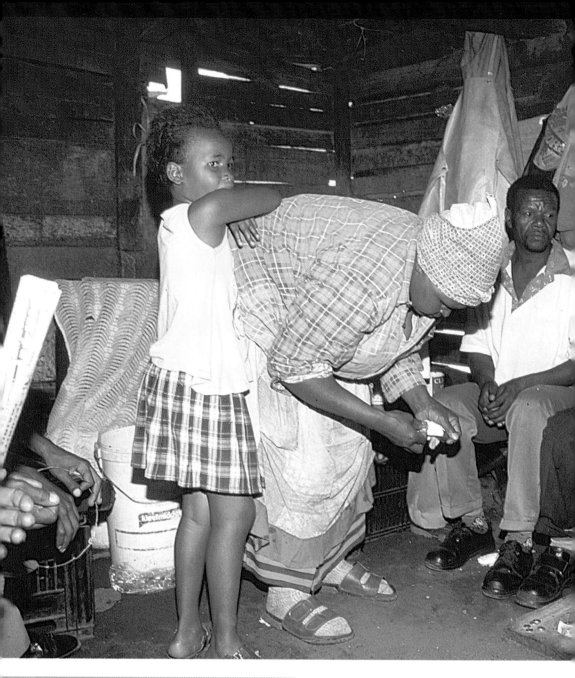

Shebeens and Taverns

During the apartheid years, blacks were forbidden to run a bar and illegal bars called **Shebeens** emerged without license or official permission. They served and still serve a special social purpose in the townships. The shebeens are usually tiny wooden hovels, and old crates are used as seats. The only available drink, the traditional Umgqombothi, is brewed in big barrels behind the hut by the bar lady herself. The milky, cloudy beer is not only affordable but also nutritious. One does not simply drink *Umgqombothi* by oneself as it is a community ritual. The men meet in the shebeen and either sit down on a box or kneel down as they never drink while standing. If a man can afford it, he buys a bucket of Umgqomboti, four litres cost R 8,00. A customer who does not have this much, throws the coins he has into a wooden ring on the floor and others will do the same. When they have scraped together R 8,00, the woman behind the bar goes to the barrel and fills the bucket. The man who has thrown the last coin will be the first to drink

Left and bottom right: *Bucket with Umgqombothi makes the round*
Top: *Shebeens are a regular meeting point for men's affairs*
Middle: *Brew master with containers to be used for the preparation of Umgqombothi*

and then passes the bucket on to his right hand neighbour, regardless of whether he has given any money or not. Each man takes the bucket, joggles it a little in order to bring the best parts of the beer up, wipes his lips, turns the bucket a little to drink from another spot and swallows with great relish. Each, in turn, passes the bucket to his right hand neighbour. According to an old Xhosa tradition, everything is to be shared,so it doesn't matter if one has money or not, everyone is equal and part of the community, Ubuntu.

More **exclusive shebeens** are found unexpectedly in a normal residential house, the outer appearances of which is no different from the houses next door. The front room is turned into a bar. During the time of apartheid, the women running the shebeen had to hide the beer which they carried home under their clothing. Then it was sold to the guests. Castle Lager is served in litre bottles and only for special occasions is umbqomboti brewed. In former times the Shebeens were often secret meeting places and members of the ANC came together in these illegal bars to discuss their next steps and actions in their fight for liberation.

Today these bars are tolerated but not supported by the authorities which see them as a stumbling block in the fight against alcoholism in the Townships. Among the residents, however, they are still very popular. For example, Tandi's Shebeen in Guguletu is the most-frequented one in the region, since she has a pool table where one can play two games for R2.00.

Top: *Tandi's shebeen*
Above: *A customer enjoying a game of pool*

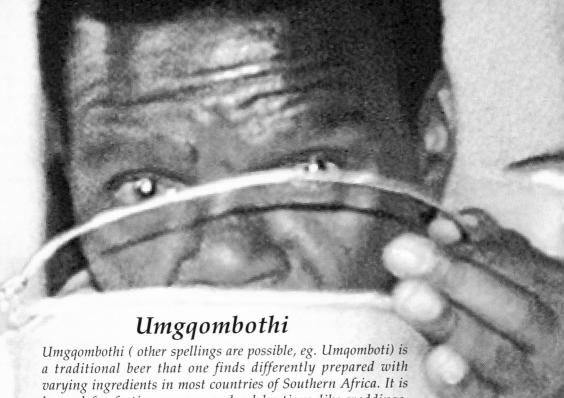

Umgqombothi

Umgqombothi (other spellings are possible, eg. Umqomboti) is
a traditional beer that one finds differently prepared with
varying ingredients in most countries of Southern Africa. It is
brewed for festive reasons and celebrations like weddings,
initiations, birthdays or funerals, and also when guests are
expected. It is the only drink offered in traditional shebeens.
Because of its high maize meal content it is very nutritious
and for the customers often the only food for the day. One can
find this beer bottled or in cans but it is best freshly prepared. In
the Cape the following recipe is being used:

Ingredients:
Mielie meal (Fine Maize meal)
Geminated maize kernels, dried and crushed
Umthombo Malt Sorghum (tropical millet sort)

   All ingredients are mixed with lukewarm water and put in a
warm place for one day. Then it is boiled. Bigger quantities are
prepared in a barrel and brought to cooking on an open fire. After
cooling, some more Umthombo is added for better fermentation.
Then it has to stand for one to three days, depending on the outside
temperature which influences the rate of fermentation. After
fermentation is completed, it is put through a woven, hose shaped
sieve, the Intlozo. It still has to settle for approximately one hour
before it can be served. The consumption of this beer is a ritual.
It is always done in a group, drunken out of a big bowl or even
a bucket which is passed around. Once it becomes your turn and
you receive the bowl from your neighbour, it will be swirled
slightly to whirl up the loved flour components, and then put
into position for the big swig.

Taverns or bars are the official successors of the Shebeens and one can recognise them by the colourful advertising. In addition to drinks, many taverns offer a small range of groceries so that one can buy urgently needed items even in the middle of the night. Shebeens are also social meeting places, like on a friday evening, particularly when all workers have received their weekly wages, they are packed. People meet and talk about what happened during the last week.

In front of the entrance, a big barbeque is lit in the evening and meat can be bought quite cheaply at the bar and grilled outside. The loudspeakers of the tavern pour music over the barbeque and the entire neighbourhood so that one becomes totally hoarse after a half-hour of conversation.

Main pic: *Tavern in Khayelitsha*
Left: *The grill in the tavern is very popular, especially on a Friday night*
Above: *In taverns most of the beer is sold in litre bottles*

Kefu's Jazz
Pub & Grill
39 Mthawelanga Street
Ilitha Park,Khayelitsha
Tel: 021 361 0566

Popza's Place
Ny 3a - 23a
Tel: 021 633 4019/ 083 511 5529
Contact person: Popza Sakula

Yellow Door
(Hot Jazz Performances & jam sessions)
192a, Eyona Shopping Centre
Cell: 082 691 3878
Contact person: Tiny

Duma's Falling Leaves
(Township music & bookings - 021 426 4260)
Ny 147
Tel: 021 637 7978

Thuthuka Sports Cafe'
Ny 134
Tel: 021 439 2061
Cell: 082 9795 831

Pat's Tavern
Tel: 021 361 9305
16 Cekiso Str.
183 site B

Winnie's Tavern
Tel: 021 361 0525
E 694 Mcedisi Str.

Waterfront
Tel: 021 387 1745
F 699 A, Site C

ᨃ Restaurants

With the increasing number of visitors more and more **restaurants**, some of them very good, are emerging in the Townships. Khayelitsha was the trailblazer, and today one can still find most of them here. But there are also good restaurants in Langa, Guguletu and Cross Roads. The menus offer original Xhosa, Cape Malay and Township dishes.

A visit to one of the township restaurants is worthwhile for the interested customer and the lover of authentic African cuisine which is otherwise very difficult to find in Cape Town.

Victor Myuqulwa started the restaurant project **Zu Enziko.** Besides running the restaurant, he also trains cooks. Trainees of his courses stand agood chance of finding a job in the major hotel kitchens of Cape Town. Owing to generous sponsors, this project could develop into a successful undertaking. With good reason, Victor

is proud that every year he and his team are entrusted with catering for the Inauguration of Parliament. In the restaurant itself they have already welcomed President Thabo Mbeki and the Minister of Health. The manager of the restaurant, Eziko Veuswa Mbolewako, employs four graduates of the project permanently and up to ten casual workers. On the menu one finds, in addition to Cape Malay dishes, traditionalXhosa dishes like Umvuba (made of maize meal and sour milk) and Umfino (made from spinach and corn mush).

As an extra, steamed Xhosa bread, made of maize meal and maize kernels is served. The Eziko has many regular guests and we met a group of employees of First National Bank, who meet there every Wednesday. Members of the Langa Administration like to have their lunch at the **Zu Enziko** resturant as well.

Main pic: *Resturant Eziko at lunch time*

Above: *Well trained cooks works at Eziko*

Bottom: *The menu at Eziko*

Isonka Sombona - maize steamed bread

The Isonka Sombona would have traditionally been cooked in a three legged cast iron pot over a small outdoor fire. This moist and delicious bread goes well with traditional Xhosa stews and meat. While Isonka Sombona is cooked in urban Xhosa homes, it is popular in sqatter camps because it is not expensive.

Ingredients:
I kg flour
2 cups mealie meal
1 teaspoon yeast
pinch of salt
700 ml luke warm water

Dissolve salt and yeast in half a cup of luke warm water. Allow to froth. Add the dry ingredients and remaining water to the yeast mixture to form a soft dough. Knead the dough well on a lightly floured surface. Place dough in a slightly oiled bowl, cover with a dish towel and allow to rise until bread is double in size. Knock the bread out of the bowl and place into a greased enamel bowl. Leave bread in the bowl and create a double boiler by putting the bowl into a pot with a low level of water. Bring water to a boil. Cook on low heat for forty minutes with the lid closed.

Abe Bokwe, the owner of **Igugu Le Africa** (The Pride of Africa) in Khayelitsha, is an experienced professional cook who had worked in many excellent restaurants in Cape Town before he started up his own business in Khayelitsha. He says : "During my training and my twenty years of work I was able to learn from the best. I love good food and creative cooking and I can deal with all the demands of my guests, from a romantic dinner to a big party or to an international conference. I am glad that I now can invest all my energy in my own restaurant."

It is therefore no wonder that even members of parliament are habitués of his restaurant because of the traditional food and the relaxing atmosphere. Abe and his team are also very much in demand during big events. His last big job was when the catered for the Annual General Meeting of the South African Women's Soccer League.

Main pic: *Abe Bokwe, owner of* **Igugu Le Africa**
Below: *In the kitchen of the* **Igugu Le Africa**
Bottom: *Geusts enjoying the buffet*
Top right: *Sheila, the owner of* **Lelapa**
Bottom right: *Irish rugby team enjoying the buffet*

The restaurant **Lelapa** (Our Home) was opened in 2000 by Sheila and her daughter Monica in Langa. They had to alter their house for this purpose and a beautiful inner court was created. Sheila says: "Our mothers and our grandmothers worked in Cape Town households of white families of all nationalities and came in contact with the most diverse cuisines. They have brought their knowledge home and in this way elements of international and traditional cooking merged. The result is a typical township cuisine that we preserve.

"Just now, a rich hot and cold buffet is waiting for a rugby team from Ireland. Sheila's neighbour and friend Eric Dilima is owner of the travel agency "Herler Sports Tour", and he has brought these and many other visitors to Sheila. For other tour operators in Cape Town, a visit to Lelapa is a highlight as well. After the dessert, Sheila offers free stories of the townships. Helen from the UK wrote in the visitors' book: "I have been to Cape Town several times but this is the first time that I have visited a township. And you have made it something very special."

Umngqusho - Tasty samp and beans

Umngqusho is a very important part of Xhosa food culture. Many Xhosa people see Umngqusho as their most special dish, and as one that everybody loves to eat. At all events, some form of Umngqusho is prepared. Whenever people come to visit, mourn or celebrate, Umngqusho should be prepared. The cold winter months also lend themselves to the preparation of the tasty samp and beans and in squatter camps you can find people eating the affordable and nutritious Umngqusho from Monday to Sunday.

Ingredients:
2 cups samp Mealies
1 cup sugar beans
2 chopped onions
1 chilli or chicken stock cube dissolved in 1 cup of hot water
5 cups water
1 teaspoon salt
Soak samp over night. Drain samp and place it with beans in a pot. Boil until cooked and tender. Add onions, stock and salt. Cook on medium heat for 20 minutes or until thick.

Markets

Visitors searching for an African art souvenir or a small present should buy it at the markets in town like Greenmarket Square, Pan African Market or the Sunday market at Greenpoint. However, the person who wants the atmosphere of an African market should not miss a visit to the township markets. Here the inhabitants of the townships buy everyday essentials and a wide range of assorted goods and have their social centre. Most of these bustling markets are close to the bigger bus stops and the metro stations.There are many of them, all differing in size and goods.The **Nyanga** market is undoubtedly the biggest, most colourful and most interesting one. As at all markets the busiest day is Saturday.

The Nyanga market is known for its textiles. Textiles as far as the eye can see, T-shirts, socks, scarves, underwear and so forth, but traditional clothing is also sold, and this is very popular with the Xhosa women. One can also buy handicraft and needlework items, cosmetics and much more. At the old, roofed part of the market, behind the textile traders are the greengrocers. They are supplied with all the seasonal produce direct from the farms, which means their goods are always fresh and and the prices are very reasonable. The Nyanga residents buy their fruit and vegetables here, and so do the "hawkers", the street vendors and owners of the small fruit and vegetable stalls, which are to be found everywhere.

Main pic: *Textiles spread out on the Nyanga Market*

Left: *Farmers offloading and selling their products direct to the traders*

Top: *Stand with goods for sale at the Nyanga market*

Above: *Fruit and vegetables at the Nyanga market*

On the edge of the market we meet Merian Duduzile. She sells drums, from R 150.00 to R 170.00 depending on size. Her husband builds the drums from old barrels which he covers with cattle skins.

A few years ago, Magcina Maxhawa with three other women started to sell meat on the Nyanga market, in order to support her family of six children and an unemployed husband. From these early beginings the Nyanga Market has now become the biggest open **meat market** of Cape Town. The cows are bought from a nearby farm in Philippi. Grace Noluthando, a customer says: "I have bought my meat here for years and I have never had any problems. I know I always get fresh goods". The meat traders also offer as a special service spices and an open wood fire. Every customer can roast the meat immediately on the spot. This place has become a popular meeting place, and on the way home one can grill a piece of meat and discuss the latest news with the other customers. Men and women stand peacefully together although men normally do not step near the fire because cooking is a women's activity. While standing around the fire and chatting, boys come into contact with girls more easily than usual.

One can sometimes witness the preparation of a culinary Xhosa specialty, the "sheep's head". At the open fire the last bit of skin of the sheep head

Main pic: *The offer to prepare and grill your own meat is taken up by many customers*
Top: *Merian's drums can be bought at the market*
Above: *Live chickens waiting for the slaughter*
Below: *Lotto queue at the Nyanga market*

is singed, afterwards it is cooked and then grilled at open fire. This a Xhosa will choose even over that great favourite, Kentucky Fried Chicken. At the end of the market is a Lotto counter where long queues develop on Saturdays. During the era of apartheid, gambling was allowed only at Sun City and other casino complexes in the home-lands.

Since 2000 there is a government lottery, and Lotto fever has infected the whole country. Often the money for the lotto ticket is saved from the food money and gambled away in the hope of being lucky and winning big money on Saturday night.

In **Khayelitsha** there is a series of smaller markets, mostly situated at bustling crossroads or shopping centres. The biggest market in Khayelitsha we find in the Victoria Mxenge area, at the large Sanlam Shopping Centre, near the bus stop and the Metro station of Nongubela. In addition to the usual products of textiles and groceries, this market also has a special feature, a great selection of table and bed linen, as well as mattresses. A herbalist offers her medicinal herbs. Rather like the Lotto counters on Saturdays, one can find long queues at the counters at which electricity is sold, on an advance payment system similar to telephone cards. The money which is left after the weekly shopping on Fridays, the

pay day, will be spent on electricity. A weekend wouldn't be a weekend without television, soccer and Lotto results.

The **Guguletu** market is held at the Nyanga Metro station on NY3 Street. The street name NY is very rare today, as it was created during apartheid times and stands for "native yard". The bridge at the Nyanga Metro station connects the townships of Guguletu and Manenberg. In the area around the railway emerged a busy shopping centre with many shops, take-a-ways, small businesses and snack bars.

There is also a small section with fruit and vegetables, and household articles and medicinal herbs are also on offer.

he **Langa** market, also situated closed to the bus
:ation, at Washington Road is similar to the other
narkets opened the whole week. Specialties here
re the fresh chickens. They are slaughtered,
lucked and drawn on request. One can also have
nem grilled immediately. A visit to this market is
asily to combine with a short detour to the
lerbalist (see page 36), as he has his consulting
oom right opposite the bus station.

Left page: *The Guguletu market*

Top left: *The Khayelitsha market at Sanlam Centre*

Bottom left: *Display booth at Langa market*

Top right: *Queueing for electricity units*

Below: *NY. Street in Guguletu*

Nyanga Market
Cnr. Sithandatu & Great Touch Roads
Nyanga

Khayelitsha Market
Sanlam Centre
Aliam Road
Khayelitsha

Guguletu Market
Nyanga Station
NY3

Langa Market
Cnr Washington Road & Single Walk Road
Opp. the bus station

Hairdressers

The **hairdressers** with their colourful advertising sign-boards on the streets are very conspicuous in the townships of Cape Town.

Many of them started with small stalls and have worked up to considerable salons. The prices are very moderate, compared to town, and a new hairstyle costs the customer roughly a day's salary. The hairdressers do not see themselves as workmen but as artists. And they have every right to do so, considering the different artworks they create from short, frizzy hair, by using artificial hair and various other extensions.

In order to create such an elaborate hairstyle with innumerable plaits, two women often have to work up to eight hours. In this case, of course, the work is accompanied by a lot of talking, laughing, music and visits by neighbours and friends. In this way the salons become an important meeting place for idle gossip and exchanges of the latest news.

∿∿ Small business

Formal industry is hardly found in the Townships. Under apartheid, townships were created as dormitory suburbs for the workers who were needed in the factories of Cape Town. Today, people who have no job in the city try to earn a living in their townships as hawkers, street vendors or craftsmen.

During the last few years, a considerable crafters guild with its own workshops has developed, very largely as a result of the different projects for self-support. This is especially the case in Khayelitsha.

Different kinds of crafters and handymen concentrate in specific regions. The carpenters are to be found in New Way. Here numerous companies offer their services. The ready made

Main pic: *Shoemaker's shop in Khayelitsha*
Above: *"Bedding shop" in Khayelitsha*
Below: *Sweets trader supplying the craftsmen*

products are displayed at the side of the street, beds, cupboards, armchairs and sofas, some of them quite big and showy. It is also possible to order custom - made furniture or fittings. The quality of the workmanship is of a very high standard.

Some workshops have grown very large and a second floor has been added.

Only a few minutes away is a second workshop with different specialisations. In a garage they are busy welding pipes, while opposite a shoemaker in his tiny workshop attempts to mend the shoes which he has repaired several times before. His neighbour, Enes Mponzo, specialises in sewing pillows. The cushion covers are made on a sewing machine and are filled with foam flakes. They are sold for R 12.00 to R 39.00. Since this craft- centre attracts many customers, a green-grocer has opened nearby and offers meat and corn-cobs grilled on an open fire.

Left top: *Enes Mponzo in her pillow making business*

Left bottom: *Furniture factory*

Above: *Welding business in Khayelitsha*

Middle: *Second hand spare parts trader*

Below: *"Hardware supplies"*

Furniture Factory
M44 Mew Way
near Puma Intersection

Small Handyworks Centre
Cnr. Oscar Mpetha & Ntlazane Street
Khayelitsha

⩗⩗ Media

Radio Zibonele (help yourself) broadcasts from an old shipping container in Khayelitsha on the frequency 98.2fm. This station was established in 1993 by an Argentine doctor, head of a hospital in Khayelitsha. His patients often forgot to take their medicine or go to their next appointments, so he wanted to remind them with the help of this radio station. However, the authorities of the apartheid government were suspicious and did not understand this and they unceremoniously confiscated all technical installations and closed the radio. After the abolition of apartheid, the station applied for a transmission license which was given on 2 August 1995 for the first time, but only for one year. Since then, they have fought for a long-term solution to avoid the yearly

application. With the 20W transmitter it is possibleto reach 100,000 listeners within a radius of approximately six kilometers. During the first year of broadcasting, the radio was given financial support in the form of salaries for two employees. By now, the radio-station has got nine employees and finances itself with advertising. An elected Board which is made up of five men and five women watches over the programmes.

San Moni, the manager, says that her audience consists mainly of young people but ideally they would like to reach all age groups with their broadcasting. 90% of the programmes are broadcast in Xhosa, with 63% spoken contributions, the rest music. The radio is still

Main pic : *Giza Nobopha is a very popular Radio D.J*
Above and below: *Radio Zibonele in Khayelitsha*

connected with the primary idea of the founder, and not only because of the immediate vicinity of the hospital. Every Friday there is a programme with and for HIV patients, and on Saturdays a programme for disabled people.

Advertising for tobacco and alcohol is taboo. The station would love to exchange their antiquated analogue equipment for the modern digital type. They would like their own small production studio in addition to the tiny transmission room, as this would make the work much easier, but that is as unobtainable as the 100 W transmitter, which would enable them to reach Cape Town with their programme and to increase the audience tenfold.

Radio Zibonele 98,2 Fm
Shawco Building, Town 11
Khayelitsha
P.O. Box 294,
Khayelitsha 7783
Tel: 021 361 9344
Fax: 021 361 5194
Cell: 082 262 4018
E mail: zibonele@sn.apc.org
Website: www.sn.apc/radiozibonele/

The Link

AUGUST/SEPTEMBER 2001

19 First Floor, Sivuyile College, Guguletu 7750   •   Tel/Fax (021) 637-3235   •   E-mail: linknews@telkomsa.net

Origins of *The Link* newspaper

In 1997 Eric Klaas from Guguletu was admitted to Peninsula Technikon for a three-year-long National Diploma course in Journalism.

When Eric went to Pentech he was on a mission and had a community radio background. While attending classes daily at Pentech, Eric enrolled for a short course on broadcasting at Cape Technikon. After the first semester, this resident of Guguletu embarked on the idea of establishing a community radio or community newspaper for the community of Guguletu and tried to get the Tech and other members of the community involved.

On the 9th August 1997 the community newspaper called *Guguletu News* was launched. Only one edition was published

that year. Mr. Rob Mentjies, then lecturer of the Practice of Journalism was very supportive and attended the launch.

Because Eric had to cope with loads of academic work, the next copy of the *Guguletu News* appeared in June of 1998. In Guguletu, Eric resided at the back of someone's house working on a typewriter donated by Dr. Hanson from UCT.

In 1998 he moved from NY 136 to NY 130 and received a computer from St Francis High School, Langa, where he had completed his Grade 12 before going to Pentech. After June of 1998, as all students of the department were supposed to go out for inservice-training, Eric used the time to commit himself to the publication of the newspaper. Although the department did not

welcome this, Eric pressed on which forced him to lose his diploma.

When he was supposed to complete his studies in 1999, he sacrificed his diploma by embarking on the legalities of the project, and in the same year he formed an enterprise called Klaas Communications. Eric armed himself by registering with the corporation and pushed to get more editions of the newspaper published.

The newspaper was first accommodated at Uluntu, then in mid '99 at Sivuyile Technical College, Guguletu. The July edition was the first one to be published from the new address and appeared under the new name of *The Link*. The management of Sivuyile College welcomed the struggling newspaper and room 19 on the first floor became the home of *Link* newspaper.

Three editions were published and a second computer was purchased.

In 2000 the newspaper became a member of the Community Press Association of South Africa under Print Media. Because of administration and associated matters only two editions were

published in 2000 and more office equipment acquired.

This August edition is the **fourth** one in 2001, and it also marks the **fourth** anniversary of *The Link* newspaper.

If you want something to be successful, give yourself fully to it and you'll see the results.

It's not about the number of diplomas or degrees we carry or the names of the institutions we come from but about ourselves. Eric Klaas is still an undergraduate, but Klaas Communications is a registered Closed Corporation and *The Link* newspaper a member of the Community Press Association under Print Media of South Africa.

It's not about a piece of paper, people, its about us. *The Link* newspaper is currently covering the following communities: Langa, Nyanga, Guguletu, Crossroads, Phillipi, Khayelitsha and other sub-communities of the Cape Peninsula. So if you by any chance don't get copies of *The Link* newspaper, call us at 637-3235.

The business community can call Paul, Shwari, Babalwa or Anele on advertisement-related matters at the same number and Mike for editorial.

The imposing entrance to the Peninsula Technikon.

Newspapers in the Townships

In August 1997, Eric Klaas Fich and some of his fellow students of the Journalism Department at the Peninsula Technikon founded the first independent black township newspaper in Cape Town. The first edition of this newspaper, at this point the only one issued by the residents themselves, was called Guguletu News. They planned to distribute this newspaper only in Guguletu. Soon there was a volley of complaints from the other townships, who did not feel represented. So the decision was made to change the profile of the newspaper and to write for them all. The new name **The Link** emphasises that all townships are now connected with this newspaper. In 1999 the "Klaas Co-operation" was registered, and now **The Link** is an official and legal newspaper. It comes out monthly in an edition of 10,000 copies with a modest four pages. That **The Link** is still in existence and able to keep its readership against two strong competitors attests to its success.

Eric says: "We elected and support the ANC government, but it is difficult to communicate with it. We chose the medium of the newspaper to give the Cape Town townships a voice which the government cannot miss. We are here primarily for the township inhabitants: we want to inform them, and speak about their problems".

They decided, therefore, to have the office in the Sivuyele College in Guguletu. This office is open for everyone, and visitors are welcome, as they want close contact with the residents. Many people come in order to tell them about their worries or to give some tips and information. School classes come on excursions to see how a newspaper is produced.

The Klaas Co-operation has expanded over the years. A production department was opened, offering services to the public, for example professional videos of special occasions like weddings and funerals. The new Education Department has already held three courses on "Introduction to Journalism", with twenty-five participants in each.

The newspaper finances itself with advertisements of local businesses and companies. It is not easy to convince the businesses to advertise on a regular basis and so the only independent township newspaper fights for daily survival.

Two more newspapers are distributed free of charge in the townships: Vukani is published by the English daily newspaper The Cape Times and Vision by the Afrikaans newspaper Die Burger.

Left: *First edition of the link*
Above: *Eric Klaas, holding the newspaper, and his team*

Link Newspaper
Sivuyile Tourism Centre
Cnr. NY1 & NY4
Guguletu 7750
Tel: 021 637 3235

Artists and Crafters

you judge, you also must learn to forgive. Forgive others, forgive
...ations, forgive yourself. By using observation without judgement,
...e is no forgiveness necessary.

Marlo Morgan, Message From Forever

ᗢᗢᗢ Guga S'Thebe

In September 2000 Guga'sThebe, Arts and Cultural Centre was opened in Langa. This unique cultural centre was financed by the city of Cape Town and the Department of Arts of the provincial government. The modern building was designed by the architect Karen Smuts, of the CS Architect Studio in consultation with the community. Artists of the township were involved in the artistic creations on the walls. The cultural centre accommodates a steel design workshop, a photo studio, a ceramic workshop, a tailor, an exhibition hall, a studio for dramatic art, a large amphitheatre and many more projects.The Vukani Bantu Project and the Zahzeni Project are to be found here, and in both of them unemployed people are trained in different crafts. Visitors can buy the results of their work in the Guga's Thebe Centre at a sale exhibition. The manager, Nomkita Bavuma an actress herself, has only been in the job for a short time and has had little experience in running a cultural centre. This is noticeable nearly everywhere. The tables with the artwork

Main pic: *The cultural centre Guga's Thebe*

Top: *Nomkita Bavuma (centre) Guga's Thebe mangeress*

Above: *Mosiac artwork in front of the Guga's Thebe*

offered for purchase are covered, although every day many tourists visit Guga's Thebe Centre during their township tours. The walls are empty, the exhibition hall is closed. There is no schedule for exhibitions or performances in the amphitheatre. However, the drama course practises regularly and would love to give performances in the amphitheatre. Unfortunately the possibilities of this wonderful multi-functional building are not exploited at all and the explanation of missing sponsors is not convincing.

Guga's Thebe
Multi- purpose
Cultural & Recreational Centre
Washington Avenue,
Langa
Telephone: 021 695 3228

ᗰᗩ Drama

In St. Peter's Anglican Church in Mahabeni Road in Khayelitsha, we meet the eighteen year old Tindie Mzie. She leads a children's theatre group. The group meets regularly to rehearse a little play which Tindie wrote herself. We watch them practising for a while. Although the play is in Xhosa we get the impression that there is a great deal of improvising. With great concentration, the actors perform expressively and the audience follows the scenes closely. One can see that the latter would love to be on the stage too. Later on, more young spectators arrive and we are told that today is a special day for Tindie. She had received an invitation to a talent contest in Johannesburg and so she has invited many friends and acquaintances for today, and even a Marimba band she knows has promised to come. She hopes to be able to collect enough money for the ticket to Johannesburg.

After a long wait comes the first disappointment as the band did not arrive, so she performs the play all alone, without musical accompaniment. She leaves the aisle of the church, the stage where the play will take place, without closing the door completely. Silence, suddenly outside a song could be heard and Tindie strides into the room, singing. We are surprised at the full and beautiful voice this dainty, young woman has. The play is in Xhosa, so we cannot understand the words but we can make out that it is about the problems of a young girl. Tindie is acting very expressively. She is lying on the ground weeping and writhing and then suddenly jumps up, filled with rage. Her performance is impressive, as she portrays how rage and deep despair turn into hope and optimism. All the spectators are watching the scene, fascinated. The story Tindie narrates is about their problems, their worries. Later, Tindie

Main pic: *Acting group at Guga S' Thebe ampitheatre*

Top: *The children's playgroup practising in St.Peter's Church in Khayelitsha*

Bottom: *Tindie Mzie*

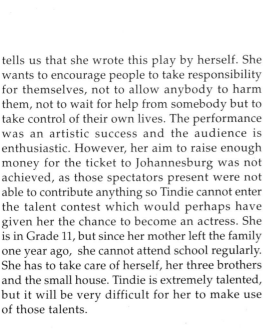

tells us that she wrote this play by herself. She wants to encourage people to take responsibility for themselves, not to allow anybody to harm them, not to wait for help from somebody but to take control of their own lives. The performance was an artistic success and the audience is enthusiastic. However, her aim to raise enough money for the ticket to Johannesburg was not achieved, as those spectators present were not able to contribute anything so Tindie cannot enter the talent contest which would perhaps have given her the chance to become an actress. She is in Grade 11, but since her mother left the family one year ago, she cannot attend school regularly. She has to take care of herself, her three brothers and the small house. Tindie is extremely talented, but it will be very difficult for her to make use of those talents.

My Life : A Story
Sadness can turn into happiness.

In the city of Cape Town, a man called Nimrod had a lover and was committed in his relationship. He lived in the shacks of Site 8 in Khayelitsha. Nimrod was a well- known man and well educated, and maintained a high standard of behaviour. You would never chat with him and come back later complaining about his attitude. He never used women.

But as time went by, his attitude towards his girlfriend changed. He even deceived her, and the saddest part was that this girl was quiet. Instead of creating a scene, she would rather go to bed. Nobody knew what had got into Nimrod.

His girlfriend cried night and day, and would have liked to know what was going on. Nimrod never confided in her but kept on dating girls and every one was shocked by his morals. However, he and his girlfriend got married, for she loved him, she believed he actually loved her and thought that this would conquer every obstacle. After they were married, things seemed to change for the better. But Nimrod's wife lost her job and he failed to support her in any way. Unfortunately, at this time she fell pregnant. There was nothing to eat and every day brought her suffering. She gave birth to a daughter. There was tension in the house, for Nimrod always reminded her that she was unemployed and insisted that she must get a job of some sort. Finally, Nimrod told her that he was leaving and that he would never come back. He went back to E-Goli where his parents lived.

Nimrod did not came back but they had an elderly woman as their neighbour, and she gave them whatever they needed. By now the baby was 16 months old and at this time the child's mother received a call from Nimrod's parents telling her that Nimrod had died of AIDS. She did not believe it. Even worse, they were accusing her of transmitting AIDS to their son and told her not to come to the funeral. The young woman could not believe that that they had said this after all she had done to make their son a good person again after his loose living.

Six month later she fell ill. She went for an HIV test and it was positive. Although she was given medication, she never used it and so she grew worse every day. Finally, she died and was buried in a government cemetery. So both parents had died of the very same disease and the books were closed on Nimrod and his girlfriend Then the elderly neighbour decided to go away and take the child with her. After sixteen years the old woman, who was dying, told the girl about her parents.

Nomalanga had grown up without knowing that the woman she was living with was not her parent. The news shocked her. She could not sleep at night and was listless during the day. She decided to go to E-Goli to look for her relatives. There was a song she used to sing when she felt sad. The song went as follows,...

Kudel Kudela	A long time ago, a long time ago
Ndihamba lonk ilizwe	I went everywhere
Ndifuna abandziyo	I'm looking for anybody who knows me
Bakuphina bakuphina	I don't know where they are.
Ndithe ndilele	One day I was sleeping
Ndaphupha umama wami	I was dreaming of my mother
Ndalala ndilele mama	I was sleeping
Ndingalele ndingalele	I was not sleeping, I was not sleeping.

When her guardian died, Nomalanga was all alone with no-one to support her. One day when she was hungry, she went to a neighbour to ask for food and this old man raped her instead of giving her something to eat. She regretted that she had ever gone to the man to beg.
Nomalanga lived on her own and earned her own living. She never found her relatives at all and they never knew that they had a grandchild. But she kept on looking all over. She worked in the ships packing fish and went to night-school and now, after all her troubles, she is a doctor.

By Tindie Mzie

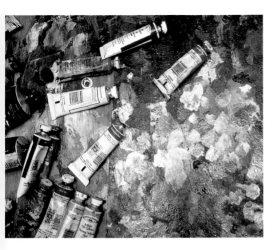

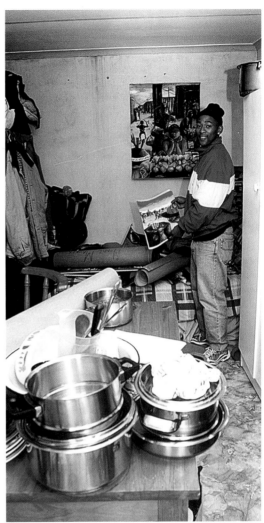

Left: *"Township life" by Moons Mahala*
Top: *The artist's utensils*
Below and right: *The artist, his house and "studio"*

Moons Mahala is twenty-eight years old. He lives in Langa and painting is his life. At the age of nine, he had already started painting and since then he has known that there is only one way of life for him, a life as a productive artist. After matriculating, he attended an art class in the Sivuyele College in Guguletu. But today he is barely able to earn a living with his paintings. In the Guga's Thebe Centre in Langa he had an exhibition but as there was no money for advertising, there were not as many visitors as expected. The newspaper "City Vision" had a report about Moons Mahala but as it is only distributed in the townships, the advertising effect was limited. He sells his pictures in Cape Town at the St.George's Mall in the open air, mainly to tourists. During the winter months, the out of season sales are very bad. Another big problem is the cramped home in which he lives and works. He says: "My spirit would be more free, I would be able to paint better pictures if I had more space".On good days he paints four or five pictures and township scenes are his favoured subject. He also tries his hand at abstract painting. But sometimes, out of economic necessity, he has to paint pictures he does not actually care for, pictures for the tourist, who will hopefully buy them.

His dream is to have an art class for children: "One can learn a lot from children, they are inspiring....". He went to the nearby Guga's Thebe Centre and offered to run an art course free of charge. Suitable premises are available and offering such courses should be the duty of the centre. But the manager sent him away saying that there was no material available and she was waiting for money from sponsors. So he has to wait for the next season and his hope is that an art connoisseur will spot one of his pictures in St. George's Mall, recognise his talent and organises an exhibition for him in Europe. Then his second dream would come true.

Mzwandine Banda Fulani is twenty-seven years old and lives in a tiny shack in Guguletu. He was the best graduate in his Matric year and started a three- year architecture diploma at the Peninsula Technikon. But after one year the urge to be an artist was stronger. He gave up his studies and participated in a one year local art project. He was able to improve his handicraft abilities and work on his technique. His brother, also an artist, is a good teacher for him. He is already well known, has given many exhibitions and has sold his pictures well. Their love for art and perhaps the talent too, comes from their father who was an amateur sculptor.

In order to show us his paintings, his girlfriend has to get up from the bed. This is the only place to sit in his hut and the pictures are stored under the mattress. One can see that he has great talent, and that one day he might become one of the important people in his field.

When we met Mzwandine, he was depressed. That morning he had received the message that a planned art exhibition in Cape Town, in which he was going to participate together with other artists, was cancelled. He had hoped to find a patron during this exhibition, who would take his pictures in part exchange so that he could buy painting materials. His dream is to have his own exhibition with his own artworks, which express all his feelings reflecting his life, his friends and his Township.

This page: *Mzwandine Banda Fulani displaying some of his artworks*

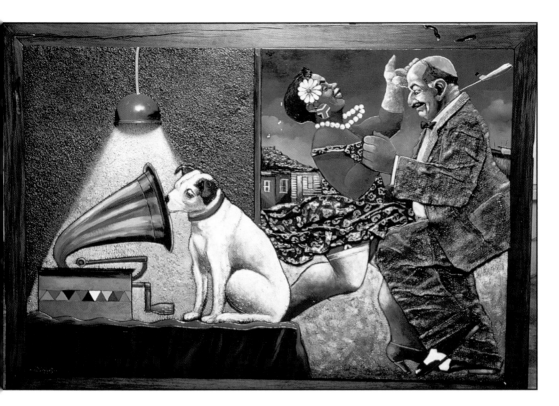

Selwin Pekeur is an artist who has managed to attain international acknowledgment. The list of his national and international exhibitions is long, and many workshops took him overseas. His art is to be found in collections around the world, including the Museum of Contemporary African Art in Washington.

He has been painting since 1980, in the beginning in his rare free time during his employment as an art teacher at a township school. In 1994, he, together with four other artists founded the art group M'Bezweni Artroup EAG. They organised exhibitions and developed young artists. In 1998 he gave up teaching in order to devote himself full-time to his art. Selwin's motto is: "Humour is the power that forges links between cultures" and so the people he paints are humorous and strong, black and white, cheerful and united.The scenes mostly show township life, and in the background is Table Mountain, the symbol of his home. In 2002 he was able to make a dream come true. In Berlin, where he made a stop on his way to an inauguration of an exhibition. He visited a Picasso and Cezanne art collection. For the first time in his life, he stood in front of the original work of his idols and was fascinated. He could not resist, he had to touch one of these originals, as he explained later, he had to let the power of the master flow into himself. The alarm went off, rousing the visitors and calling all security staff into action, but they were soon convinced that nothing serious had happened.

Now, in his latest artworks, the influence of the modern art of the Twentieth century, of Picasso and of Cezanne is to be sensed even more intensely.

This page: *Selwyn Pekeur displaying some of his artworks to the auhor*

⁓⁓ Graffiti

It's hard to imagine township life today without these spots of colour. They are to be found on walls of public places and on buildings, schools, bridges, sports grounds, taverns and many private houses. Unlike other modern Western cities, where they are in most cases only a public nuisance, here they are used as a medium to address many people. They are used to notify, and often have informative content, so the AIDS topic, for instance, plays an important role. Education in traffic regulations is done with the help of graffiti in the townships. That is very important since the inhabitants, newcomers from rural areas, do not have experience in urban traffic. Of course there are also political topics and slogans, like calls to assist in the reconstruction of the new South Africa, to make South Africa a country everyone can be proud of.

Another use of graffiti is for advertising. Whether big graffiti at taverns, inviting people to come in, or smaller pointers to specific services, all are colourful and cheerful, in most cases reminding one of Naive art. Especially conspicuous are the many Tastic rice adverts.

Some years ago an advertising agency had an idea for a special campaign, and it called for a graffiti competition. In close cooperation with local authorities, special wall spaces were selected and artists out of the communities were invited to take part. The advertising agency sponsored paint and brushes. On one weekend more than 100 advertising graffitis on the subject Tastic Rice emerged in the townships around Cape Town. A commission consisting of local representatives and the agency awarded the prizes to the best artworks.

⋀⋀ Arts and crafts

Anyone who is looking for something special for a souvenir or for his own house, and who wishes to buy directly from the producer, will certainly find what he wants in the townships of Cape Town. Most artists and craftsmen are working at various project places where they also sell their products. However, an increasing number of artisans are also getting their own workshops. It is often possible to visit the workshops and see where the chosen piece is made and by whom. The **Khayelitsha Art and Craft Market** is well known. Twenty-eight craftsmen and women display their work, and approximately three hundred visitors come each week. The project was launched by Matanzima Baleri together with Rachel Mash of St. Michael's Church. Matanzima states proudly: "This market has become our life.

Everyone who works here gives of his best because we know that one day it will pay off." In the coffee shop **Odd Cup** of the project **Learn to Earn**, one finds crafts on sale, in addition to woodworks, traditional clothing, pillows, table linen, rag dolls and much more.

In the **Tourist Information Sivuyile** in Guguletu, the products of artisans and artists can be admired and bought in the interleading curio shop, traditional clothing, pictures made with real talent, marvellous pottery and vases and coloured crockery in the African design of Sonwabo Mayford Dunyaw. Dunywa is a positive example of a successful township career. After completing a training course in business skills, he founded the company **Uncedo Pottery Project** and now he exports abroad and trains ceramists.

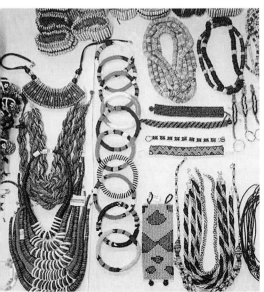

Main pic: *Dolls and their dresses on display at the Zenzele centre*

Left and above: *Products to be sold at the Khayelitsha craft market*

Top: *Khayelitsha craft market*

Middle: *Uncedo pottery project*

A specialty of the small **Guga S'Thebe Craft Market in Langa** is traditional bead work, African shirts and the trash art of Patrick. The latter repertoire includes tables, candle sticks and lamps in noble rust design. In the **Philani Nutrition Centre** in Khayelitsha one can get woven tapestries with township scenes, pillows of breath-taking beauty, shirts and other textiles. This project was started in 1998 by the Swedish doctor Ingrid le Roux, who is still working in Khayelitsha. During a visit one can watch the women weaving, see the kindergarten, also a part of the project, or meet **Gocini hit Mphathi**, the designer of the extraordinary textiles in Khayelitsha, and it is possible to buy cute rag dolls.

In the **Zenzele Centre** in Walter Sisulu Road there are also very beautiful shirts, which will be custom-made on request. Since this centre is very close to the restaurant **I Gugu Le Africa**, it is possible to combine these transactions with a tempting meal.

Also near by is **Kwa-Noothemba**, the workshop for the disabled. There are wooden artefacts and pretty items of handmade paper to see and buy. Using old newspapers and computer paper, the physically-challenged make papier-mâché and out of this they create new greeting-cards with African motifs, sheets of writing paper, envelopes and other things. The typical irregularities and the uneven surface of

the paper give the products a very special and unique attraction. Seeing the enthusiasm of the people while doing their work and their pride while offering their products, makes choosing and buying even more joy. After an exhausting day of shopping, it is time for a little breather. That is possible in the beautiful garden of the **Home Management Training Centre Zanokhanhyo** where one can relax on benches in the open air, enjoying a delicious piece of cake baked at the in-house bakery and drinking a nice cup of coffee. This is a project of the Catholic church where women are trained in housekeeping so eventually they will be prepared to work in hotels, guesthouses or private households.

Left page: *Carpet Weaver at Philani Centre*
Top: *Disabled people at Kwa-Noothemba*
Left: *Bakery at Zanokhanyo Centre*
Above: *Tapestry ready for sale*

Something very special is offered by **Sonwabo Nongawuza**, called **Golden**. In 1991 he came with his family to Khayelitsha and began to make flowers from old cold- drink cans. Although his English is very poor and he works on his own in his small workshop, he is becoming famous. The artist Annie Bisseb of Wynberg was so enthusiastic about his flowers and his warmth that she painted his portrait in 1999 and gave it to him as a present. Sally Argent wrote a little story about Golden and his dream(see yellow Box). His tin flowers are very popular with locals and tourists, and in the Cape Town markets his creations are very much in demand. These flowers are even wanted abroad.

In 2001 he delivered 2000 pieces to New Zealand and 400 to Germany. His production capacity is about 25 to 30 flowers per day. It is an excellent job and enables him to provide a good life for his family of eight.

Comprehensive lists of the artists and further information and tips are available in the Tourist Information Centres of Khayelitsha and Guguletu. It does not matter what or where someone buys on the township markets, any purchase directly supports a non-profit project or an artist without extensive distribution channels, and gives financial and moral support and further incentive to them and to many other township inhabitants.

This page: *Golden's beautiful flower creations*
Next page: *Golden in his workshop*

Sonwabo Nongawuza (Golden)

There was once a man called Golden who came to live in Cape Town. He had a wife called Phumla and a family of five daughters but he had no home and no work. They settled in the sprawling squatter camp called Khayelitsha outside the city and built themselves a shack. Phumla started a crèche, caring for the neighbourhood children, and Golden went in search of a job. But work was scarce and the family was often hungry. One night Golden had a dream. He dreamed of a rubbish dump filled with flowers, yellow and white, and a voice told him to pick and sell and he would have money for food. On awaking, Golden hurried to the dump, but though he searched from end to end, he found no flowers. The next night he had the same dream. Again he went in search of flowers but returned home disappointed and empty handed. On the third night the dream came again. He was sure it was the voice of God. But where were the flowers? Why could he not find them? For the third time Golden walked to the dump. This time, in the course of searching, he noticed piles of empty soft-drink cans, yellow and white. Suddenly he understood. He gathered up a few cans and hurried home. In the shack he set to work with a pair of scissors and a pot of paint. After many setbacks he finally fashioned a flower just like the ones in his dream: a perfect daisy with a long green stem, pointed white petals and a yellow centre. Now Golden makes flowers from other people's waste and sells them to make a living. As well as daisies, he now makes roses and sunflowers. He makes each one himself, by hand.

(reprinted with friendly permission of Sally Argent)

Khayelitsha Craft Market
St Michael's Church, Khayelitsha- Harare
Monday - Thursday 9.00 am - 2.30 pm
Tel/ Fax: 3615246
Uncedo Pottery Project,
Sivujele Centre, Guguletu
Monday – Friday: 9.00 am – 5.00 pm
Tel: 6335461 /Fax: 6377638
Golden's Tin Flowers,
Khayelitsha
Malandalahla Cresent
(second corner left hand site with a blue wooden gate)
Zenzele Training Centre,
Khayelitsha
Cnr. Spine Rd/ Walter Sisulu Rd.
Monday – Friday: 9.30 am – 4.00 pm
Tel: 361 1975

Kwa – Nothemba,
Mitchells Plain
PoBox 494
Mitchells Plain, 7785
Monday – Friday: 9.30 am – 4.00 pm
Tel. 361 1560
Zanokhanyo,
Khayelitsha - Harare
Crn. Qamela Rd/ Fumana Rd
Monday – Friday: 10.00 am – 4.00 pm
Tel: 363 1782
Fax: 363 0392
Philani,
Khayelitsha
Walter Sisulu Rd, Site C
Monday – Friday: 9.30 am – 4.00 pm
Tel: 387 5124
Fax: 387 5170

Tour operators offering township tours

Company	Tel. no.	Fax no.	Cell no.	E-mail address
Cape Capers Tours	021 4483117	021 4483117	083 3580193	tourcape@mweb.co.za
South African Safu Touring	021 5118557	021 5118557	072 1202074 073 2385569	satuks@telkomsa.net
Meljo Tours	021 9046634	021 9046634	082 8204946	info@meljotours.com
Grassroute Tours	021 7061006	021 7050798		grasrout@iafrica.com
GCT Tours	021 6919192	021 6919192	082 9685636	gctours@mweb.co.za
Legend Tourism	021 6974056/7	021 6974090		info@legendtourism.co.za
Roots Africa Tours	021 9878330	021 9885641	082 2549092	rootsafrica@xsinet.co.za
Ubuntu Tours		021 5055697	073 1862926	
Alternative Township Tour	021 8870590	021 8838019	083 3360342/ 083 7403583	
Caleb	021 4245509	021 4230448		janet@calebcon.co.za
Bouraque		021 4221415	083 7261110	bouraque@altavista.com
Our Pride Tours	021 5314291	021 5314291	082 4467974	ourpride@ mweb.co.za
Deovolente Tours		021 9191364	083 4608048	capett@netactive.co.za
Sherwood Tours	021 5585573	021 5585573	083 3635933	mikemar@telkomsa.net
Ezizwe Travel &Tours	021 6970068	021 4393214	082 7131975	mwezizweqmweb.co.za
African Eagle	021 4644266	021 4476300	082 4771898	email
Hozani Tours	021 5550400	021 5550408	083 7150473, 083 4605574	daytour@aecpt .co.za info@hozanitours.co.za
Cape Team Tours		021 9034638		
Cape Rainbow Tours	021 5515465	021 5515216	083 3106454	caperainbow@iafrica.c
AfriCultural Tours	021 4233321		082 9675203	
Cosmos Tours	021 9101677			
Elwierda Tours	021 4184673	021 9513378		
Geometric Tours	021 9513378	021 6338378	072 2427839	
Kuyasa Shuttle and Tours	021 6338378	021 5314293	082 7469444	
Bonani our Pride Tours	021 5314293		083 9526084	
Khwela Khwela Tours	021 3876612			